HOW TO SAY IT

Creating Complete Customer Satisfaction

HOW TO SAY IT

Creating Complete Customer Satisfaction

Winning Words, Phrases, and Strategies
to Build Lasting Relationships in Sales and Service

JACK GRIFFIN

Prentice Hall Press

PRENTICE HALL PRESS
Published by the Penguin Group
Penguin Group (USA) Inc.
375 Hudson Street, New York, New York 10014, USA

USA / Canada / UK / Ireland / Australia / New Zealand / India / South Africa / China

Penguin Books Ltd., Registered Offices: 80 Strand, London WC2R 0RL, England
For more information about the Penguin Group, visit penguin.com

Library of Congress Cataloging-in-Publication Data

Griffin, Jack.
How to say it : creating complete customer satisfaction : winning words, phrases, and strategies to build
lasting relationships in sales and service / Jack Griffin.
p.   cm.
Includes bibliographical references and index.
ISBN 978-0-7352-0525-3 (alk. paper)
1. Selling.   2. Customer services.   3. Consumer satisfaction.   4. Business communication.   I. Title.
HF5438.G8837   2013
658.8'12—dc23   2012040877

First edition: March 2013

PRINTED IN THE UNITED STATES OF AMERICA

10   9   8   7   6   5   4   3   2   1

Text design by Tiffany Estreicher

While the author has made every effort to provide accurate telephone numbers, Internet addresses, and
other contact information at the time of publication, neither the publisher nor the author assumes any
responsibility for errors, or for changes that occur after publication. Further, the publisher does not have
any control over and does not assume any responsibility for author or third-party websites or their content.

Most Prentice Hall Press books are available at special quantity discounts for bulk purchases for sales
promotions, premiums, fund-raising, or educational use. Special books, or book excerpts, can also be
created to fit specific needs. For details, write: Special Markets, Penguin Group (USA) Inc.,
375 Hudson Street, New York, New York 10014.

To Flora

CONTENTS

Part Three: Speak the Language of Complete Satisfaction

PREFACE

Like my other How to Say It books, *How to Say It: Creating Complete Customer Satisfaction* provides practical, results-oriented guidance for effective communication, with emphasis on words, phrases, scripts, and strategies applied to real-world examples and scenarios.

In contrast to the vast majority of books that deal with customer communication, *How to Say It: Creating Complete Customer Satisfaction* does not separate sales from customer service communications, but instead integrates the two fields into a single book. This innovative approach is intended to directly engage the current realities of business in two key dimensions:

1. Increasingly, firms are merging or at least overlapping sales and service functions. As e-commerce tends to level the field in terms of pricing and availability, more companies are promoting service as a value added to distinguish their offerings from those of others. Sales professionals are therefore increasingly expected to address customer service issues rather than hand them off to a separate Customer Service Department. For their part, Customer Service personnel are increasingly expected to guide customer purchases, especially in the areas of upgrading, upselling, and promoting customer communities. The current

reality is that the wall between sales and service is becoming more and more porous.

2. The growing overlap of sales and service reflects an emerging definition of the customer not as a person who sometimes needs to be sold to and at other times needs to be attended to with service, but as someone who must be satisfied—*at all times*.

How to Say It: Creating Complete Customer Satisfaction is a book for anyone today who has, who needs, who needs more, and who does not want to lose, customers. It is a book for the new business reality that volumes focused exclusively on sales or service do not adequately address. It is a book about using language to create satisfaction in the *whole* customer *all the time* and in *every phase* of the sales-service cycle.

PART ONE

SPEAK THE LANGUAGE OF YES

The six chapters that follow will teach you the essential language of sales and service, including how to prepare yourself to communicate in ways that always address the customer's needs and wants, how to identify prospective customers, and how to develop a vocabulary of value. You will also learn the time-tested AIDA formula for making a sale and creating a loyal customer; you will learn to welcome resistance and convert it into a selling opportunity; and you will master the all-important art of the close.

CHAPTER 1

Prepare Yourself

You've probably heard about it. Maybe it's even happened to you. You get asked the infamous "sell me this pen" job interview question. It goes like this: You apply for a sales job, and you snag an interview. Now you're sitting face-to-face with the boss. Suddenly, she takes a pen from her desk and hands it to you.

"Sell me this pen," she says.

What do you do?

Your first impulse is to object that you don't know anything about this particular brand of pen. *So how can I sell it? A salesperson has to know the product, right? How can I sell something that's just been handed to me?*

But you resist the impulse to protest. (Good thing, too. You really want the job.) Instead, you scramble to make stuff up about the pen. You invent a feature. You comment on the style. You talk about the price. If you can tap-dance like this for three or four minutes, you may even create a favorable impression. After all, the question didn't make you go blank, which is what would happen to a lot of people. Will the tap dance be enough to get you the job? Maybe, provided you don't sweat too much or start to look sick or gaze down at the floor, the ceiling, and every place but the other person's eyes.

Maybe just the ability to say *something* and to look reasonably convincing will be enough.

Maybe. Probably not.

There is a better approach.

WHAT IS SELLING?

If you've been selling for a while, you understand the importance of asking questions. Even if you are brand-new to selling, you certainly have experience buying, and you know that a good salesperson focuses on you, never on himself. He focuses on your needs, wants, problems, and requirements. He discovers these by asking questions, then he sells you the product in response to your answers.

A failed salesperson will *tell* you: "Buy this car. I need the commission to make my mortgage this month." It is an honest, straightforward appeal, but it has nothing to do with *your* needs and everything to do with *his*. That is why it is the approach of a failed salesperson.

A successful salesperson (or at least a *more* successful salesperson) will *ask* you: "So what's more important to you, zero-to-sixty acceleration or a lot of miles to the gallon?" Using your answer, he will begin to sell you cars that address your need, whether it is for performance or for economy or for some combination of the two.

"Sell me this pen."

So you answer with a question: "What do you look for in a pen?"

She's handed you a 98-cent throwaway. Now, you might get lucky. She might answer your question with something like "Cheap price. Under no circumstances do I want to pay more than a dollar for a pen." In this case, you can close the sale by saying, "I can let you have this one for ninety-eight cents." If, however, she answers, "Elegance. I need a pen that announces me as successful and elegant," you are in trouble. The 98-cent merchandise you have in your hand does not even begin to satisfy her requirements as set forth in her answer to your question.

What you've undoubtedly heard from veteran sales professionals is absolutely right. Successful sales are all about asking questions. But you must be certain to ask the questions to which you already have the *salable* answers. We'll get to that later. There is, however, a question you have to ask yourself first—right now, in fact. You have to ask it and answer it and repeat the question-and-answer sequence from now on at least every few days of every week of your selling career, no matter how long that may turn out to be.

The question is *What is selling?*

One obvious answer is *The act, art, or skill of persuading someone to hand you money in exchange for a product or service.*

That is certainly an accurate description of selling, but it does not address what we may call the essence or the heart of selling: the force that drives a successful sale time and time again.

What is selling?

Selling is satisfying a need at a price.

That, anyway, is the start of it. You may have to begin by showing, proving, demonstrating, or persuading the prospect that he has a need that requires satisfaction. You may even have to go so far as to create a need.

"Sell me this pen."

In response, you reach into your jacket pocket and pull out your checkbook. You write a check. "How do you spell your last name?" you ask. Handing over the check, you say: "Here's a check for twenty dollars. I'll honor it, provided you endorse it now, right now, in my presence."

Your prospective employer looks at you, blankly.

Now you ask the question about need, a question to which you know the answer because *you* have created the need: "Don't you wish you had a pen right now?"

SELLING IS SATISFYING A NEED AT A *FAIR* PRICE

Consider the sentence *Selling is satisfying a need at a price.* You could express it as an equation:

Selling = Satisfaction divided by Price

Assign a numerical value to Satisfaction and a numerical value to Price somewhere between 1 and 3. The "correct" solution is one in which Selling is a value of 1 or greater:

$1 = 1 \div 1$ is "correct"—that is, a successful sale, because the value of the Satisfaction appears to be exactly proportionate to the Price that is being demanded for it. The customer is satisfied—or will be, once he hands over the money and receives the product or service. "I need it, and it's priced fairly," he says to himself.

$0.5 = 1 \div 2$ is "incorrect"—that is, an unsuccessful sale, because the value of the Satisfaction appears to be less than the Price that is being demanded for it. The customer is not satisfied and does not think she will ever be satisfied, so she holds on to her money. "It's not worth it. I don't really need it."

$1.5 = 3 \div 2$ is "correct." In fact, it is a *highly* successful sale, because the value of the Satisfaction appears to be more than the Price that is being demanded for it, and yet the Price is sufficient to create a profit and thereby sustain the business.

At *minimum*, selling is satisfying a need at a *fair* price. At an *optimum* level, selling is satisfying a need at a "good" price, a "great" price, a "bargain" price.

OPTIMUM SELLING MAKES BOTH YOU AND YOUR CUSTOMER RICHER

If the *minimum* requirement is met, the customer will anticipate feeling that, while he has parted with some money, the sacrifice was a fair one. If the *optimum* level is reached, however, the customer will feel that, although he has parted with some money, he is actually the richer for having done so. Receiving his money, you will also feel richer. In fact, you will feel rich beyond the cash now in your hand. In addition to possessing the money, you will feel the priceless satisfaction of having created satisfaction, of having made both your customer and yourself richer. That is optimum selling.

SATISFY YOURSELF

Say the word *salesman* to most people, ask them to respond with the first thing that comes to their mind, and odds are you won't like what you hear. *Crook*, *cheat*, and *sleazeball* will be some of the more polite responses.

It doesn't have to be this way. If you can consistently make optimum sales, creating in your customer the feeling that by spending money to acquire the product or service you presented to her she has not diminished her wealth but increased it, you will create many positive associations with the word *salesman*. You will feel good, very good, about what you do.

For too long, we have been willing to accept as an unalterable fact that selling is a zero-sum game, in which the salesperson wins only if the customer loses. Money changes hands, moving from the customer's to that of the salesperson. The customer's loss is the salesperson's gain.

This situation accurately describes a $0.5 = 1 \div 2$ sale, that is, an unsuccessful sale. It is possible—though not likely—for a salesperson to scrape by on nothing but such sales. Yet even if he does manage to avoid the unemployment line transacting this kind of business, he can hardly be called a successful salesperson. A *successful* sales professional does not merely make one-shot sales, she creates customers, satisfied customers, who will recommend what she sells to others and who will buy more of it themselves. *Sales made* without creating satisfaction do not build a sustainable, let alone a growing, business. *Customers created* do.

SELF-TALK

A sustainable business can probably be created by consistently selling perceived value in return for perceived value: $1 = 1 \div 1$. If you want to do more than sustain your business, if you want to grow it, you must consistently sell higher perceived value for lower perceived value: $1.5 = 3 \div 2$. It's what people commonly call "good value" or "great value for the money." Achieve this, and you will feel satisfied in your profession.

But now we come to a "chicken and egg" question. Do you have to achieve high-value sales that create great customer satisfaction before *you* can feel satisfied, or must *you* feel good about who you are and what you do before you can achieve a high level of success? The answer is that the relationship between your feelings and your performance should be—and *can* be—a virtuous circle.

The familiar phrase "vicious circle" describes a relationship in which one negative feeds another: You feel bad about being in sales, therefore you produce poor and unsatisfying sales, which, in turn, make you feel even worse about being in sales. A *virtuous circle* is just the opposite: You feel good about your profession and therefore produce satisfying sales, which make you feel even better about what you do and who you are.

Position yourself for entry into a virtuous circle by reflecting on your inner dialogue, the continual mental conversation in which all of us engage. Now, take steps to purge any negative internal chatter you hear and convincingly replace it with positive self-talk. Here's how:

1. Become Aware of Your Inner Conversation.

Listen to yourself think. It takes some deliberate concentration, but you can do it. Very likely, you will be amazed at the volume of negativity that flows through your mind. Do you hear yourself complaining? Do you hear yourself expressing regret? Do you call yourself stupid or clumsy or unlucky? Is your self-talk full of worry? Are you continually cautioning yourself, warning yourself away from taking any risk? Is your inner dialogue pretty much devoted to self-criticism?

If you try to answer these questions, you will find yourself becoming increasingly aware of your negative self-talk. Now, once you become aware of it, respond to it. If you find yourself saying "That was stupid of me," respond with: "Was it really?" If you can't answer that with an unequivocal yes, chances are you did not act stupidly or, at least, not as stupidly as you think. If you can answer it yes, then ask, "What should I do differently next time?" If you can correct a mistake or avoid making another one, you're smarter than most.

Challenge every negative piece of self-talk similarly. "I better not take a chance on trying that." Respond with: "Why shouldn't I?" Or: "I can't do that." Respond, "Why not?" or, even more directly, "Yes, I can."

Question and disrupt your automatic, unthinking stream of negative self-talk.

2. Set Goals. State Them Positively.

Formulate goals, both long-term and daily. Formulate them in short declarative sentences. "I will close three sales today." "I will learn the features and benefits of the new models backward and forward." Give yourself specific tasks to accomplish. Make achievement something measurable. You will feel better about yourself when you prove to yourself that you can set a goal and achieve it.

3. Visualize the Outcome You Want.

Make up a story about your day. Give it a happy ending. Visualize success on a daily basis. Imagine yourself selling more in a day than the best salesperson in your department sells in a week. Tell yourself the story of those sales. Explain to yourself how you made each one of them. Tell yourself what it feels like: what *success* feels like.

4. Swap Negative Influences for Positive Ones.

Find some inspirational stories to read or uplifting movies to see. Avoid the downbeat and the negative. If your best buddies are pessimists, you need to find some enthusiastic, cheerful, energetic folks to hang with. Perform an emotional face-lift. Redecorate your life with everything that is motivating. Set aside the discouraging.

5. Live in the Present.

Don't chew over the past, and try not to worry about the future. Instead, focus on what you can do in the present. When your energy or commitment begins to flag, ask yourself point-blank: "What can I do *right now*?" Get your arms around the present. Grapple with it. Shape it. Work with it.

6. Deal with Your Fears.

Take a fear inventory. List what you are afraid of. Put it in writing, one item after another, a separate numbered line for each item. The mere act of verbalizing and organizing your fears this way will cut them down to size. Now confront each of them, one by one. For each fear, ask: What is the worst that can happen as a result of this item? Break each fear down into its causes and realistic effects, then formulate a plan of action for each fear. Take each in turn. Write everything down.

7. Take a Mental Vacation.

Give yourself permission to feel good. Picture your favorite place and favorite people. Imagine yourself there and with them. What does the place look like? What surrounds you? What does it sound like? Smell like? Feel like? What do you and the others talk about? Put yourself there. Enjoy yourself. Do this at least five times every day.

Replacing your negative inner dialogue with a more positive mental conversation won't take a minute or an hour or a day. In fact, it will take at least twenty-one days, assuming you practice converting the negative to the positive on each and every one of those days. Recent research suggests that it requires, on average, twenty-one days to create a habit or replace one habit with another. Create the good habit of positive self-talk, and you will find yourself happier, more energetic, more positive—and more capable of producing excellent results in whatever you undertake, including satisfying customers with top-level sales and superb service. Achieve this level of success, and you will feel even better about yourself and your profession. The circle will have morphed from vicious to virtuous.

APPLY POSITIVE SELF-TALK

Once you have acquired the habit of positive self-talk, apply it to preparation for the mission of selling whatever you have to sell.

Replace Negative Feelings About Your Merchandise with Positive Affirmations About It

It is difficult, discouraging, and depressing to try to sell products and services in which you have little faith or confidence. Typical negative feelings about your merchandise may include:

1. It's a poor value—not worth the price.
2. People don't really need it.
3. It's not as good as I have to say it is.
4. People should save their money instead of wasting it on stuff like this.

Now, identify the positive features, benefits, and value of what you sell. Sell the merchandise to yourself. Don't stop selling until you can convert the negatives to outright affirmations:

1. My merchandise delivers extraordinary value. It isn't the cheapest, but it *is* the greatest value.
2. My merchandise is of great use and benefit to my customers. I serve them well by introducing it and selling it to them.
3. My merchandise is better than most people think. My job is to tell my customers just how much better it is.
4. My customers are enriched by my products.

You also need to feel good about the organization for which you work. Negative chatter about one's workplace is common—almost automatic, in fact. Breathe deeply, blink your eyes, and take the opposite approach. Broadcast the good news about where you work:

1. My company is the best in the business.
2. My company delivers even more than it promises.
3. I am proud to work for my company.
4. My company values its customers and creates total customer satisfaction.

SPEAK THE LANGUAGE OF HIGH-VALUE SELLING

Perception is all we really know about the reality around us, and words shape perception; therefore, learn to speak the language that will produce the most favorable perceptions when it comes to selling. Consider the words and phrases to avoid and those to use.

PREPARING TO SELL: NEGATIVE WORDS AND PHRASES TO AVOID

Barebones	Nobody can do that
Bargain-priced	Nobody can satisfy everybody
Cheap	Not worth it
Costly	Outsourced
Expensive	Overpriced
Experimental	We aren't trying to compete with
Frills	their prices

PREPARING TO SELL: AFFIRMATIVE WORDS AND PHRASES TO USE

Best	Finest
Breakthrough product/service	Innovative
Commitment to service/value	Investment in service
Customized for you	Let's talk about value, not cost
Deliver high value	Most effective
Excellence	Newest

Problem solver
Solution
The standard
This is the best we've ever
    designed
Unrivaled in the industry
Value proposition
We are proud of this product

We can expedite that
What you need
What you want
Whatever you want
You will be pleasantly surprised
    by the price
You will be satisfied

CHAPTER 2

Go Prospecting

The most surprising thing all sales professionals have in common is that all of them own just one item of inventory. If you're selling cars, the dealership owns the inventory of sedans, SUVs, and trucks. If you're selling vacuum cleaners, the store you work for owns every single machine. If you're selling life insurance, underwriters finance the works. Like every other salesperson on the planet, all you have on your personal stock shelves is your time. That and only that is your inventory. Don't lose it. Don't give it away. Exchange it as any other inventory asset is exchanged: only for value received.

You meet a new person. She asks you what you do. You say you're in sales.

"Oh," she responds, "I have a cousin who can sell a lump of coal to a coal miner."

And that's myth number one: *A good salesperson can sell anything to anyone.* All you can say about this is that it's simply not true, no truer than saying, "A good doctor can cure anybody." Obviously, in the first place, the patient has to have something to be cured. Second, that something has to be curable. Similarly, a good salesman needs a good customer—one who needs or wants what he's selling and one who has the means and authority to purchase it.

Myth number one is related to myth number two: *Sales is just a matter of numbers.* The assumption is that the more prospects you approach and the greater your endurance, the more you will sell. To a limited degree, this is true. But selling by numbers alone is never going to be efficient enough to make you a living. You just don't have the inventory—the time—to squander on one dead-end prospect after another.

And so myth number two leads to myth number three: *All prospects are equal.* The fact is that some have no interest in what you have to sell and never will. Some are interested but have neither the funds nor the authority to buy. Some are inveterate window-shoppers. Some are too price-sensitive for your line. Some may buy once but will never give you repeat business, so, depending on what you are selling, they may not be strategically worth the investment of your time.

Prospecting for customers does not mean just finding people who exhibit a pulse. It means avoiding the wrong prospects—who will waste your time, the only precious inventory you own—and identifying and investing your time with qualified prospects who are ready to buy. This chapter will help you to connect with them.

GENERATE LEADS AND QUALIFY PROSPECTS

An old-time gold prospector used a pan or a pick and shovel. All you need is a sturdy acronym. It's BANT—B-A-N-T—and it stands for *Budget, Authority, Need,* and *Timing.*

Budget. Identify prospects who have the means, the budget, to buy what you are selling. If a prospect has any or all of the other qualifying prerequisites but not the *Budget*, you are wasting your inventory of time engaging with her. Move on.

Authority. When contacting a given organization, you are likely to run into any number of perfectly nice, polite, and helpful people. Be kind and courteous to them all, but recognize that only one is absolutely crucial to making the sale. He is the person with the *Authority* to buy what you are selling. Identify the decision maker. In some organizations, this will be a "C-level" executive—CEO, CTO, CFO—in others, it will be a purchasing manager, an office manager, and so on. Identify whatever person has the authority to buy. Target him.

Need. Determine, preferably by advance research but, if on-site, as soon as possible, what the prospect's *Need* for your product or service is. Don't get me wrong. One thing an effective salesperson does is educate and persuade a prospect to understand and accept his *Need* for what you sell. But you must understand the limits of possibility. A carpenter can be persuaded to buy the high-end titanium handsaw you offer. A baker? Almost certainly not.

Timing. Timing, especially where substantial purchases are concerned, can be critical to making the sale or not. Research the industry and the customer. If you know that XYZ Company needs to show a substantial fourth-quarter profit to its investors, wait until the first quarter of next year to sell them your high-end widget. The company's leadership is not likely to be in the mood to make a big-money purchase just now. On the other hand, if you know that XYZ has just signed a contract to fill a big order, that high-end widget might be just what the company needs right now to do the job. Pounce.

Where you get your leads depends on the market into which you are selling. It is your business to learn where the customers are and who they are. But one thing is true of all markets, all industries, and all classes of consumer: Your best prospects are your current customers. Start with them before prospecting in fresh fields.

When you get a lead on someone, be sure to take time to understand just what role that person plays in the organization you are approaching. Typically, the prospect you contact plays one or more of four roles:

1. *Gatekeeper.* A lot of administrative assistants and similarly titled individuals play the role of gatekeeper. Their primary responsibility is to keep you out.
2. *User.* This is the person or persons who will actually use the merchandise you are selling.
3. *Buyer.* The decision maker—the individual who actually makes the purchase and writes the check. In some situations, when dealing directly with a solo operator or owner, this is the only prospect you will deal with. In larger organizations, chances are that you will encounter a gatekeeper and perhaps a user first.
4. *Champion.* Look for these. They are individuals within the organization who can help you make the sale, typically by leading you to the *user(s)* and *buyer* and by advocating your product to them.

EXAMPLES

Speaking with a Gatekeeper
You call. You hear:

GATEKEEPER: Hello, Jane Small's office. This is Art. How may I help you?

YOU: Good morning, Art. I recently spoke with Ms. Small's associate, Pete Campbell, who thought I could help Ms. Small with a purchase. I'm following up, and I'm hoping you can connect us.

GATEKEEPER: Let me see if she is available.

YOU: Thank you, Art.

If the gatekeeper connects you with your prospect, great! If not, do your best to recruit the gatekeeper as an ally:

GATEKEEPER: Ms. Small is in a meeting.

YOU: I see. Art, I wonder if you can help me. Pete Campbell was very specific about Ms. Small's needs, and I do think she will want to hear what we can offer. What would be the best time for me to call again?

GATEKEEPER: You could try later this afternoon—around three.

YOU: Terrific. Thanks. Could you, please, jot down my name, Ben Wilson of XYZ Corporation? And, if you will, make a note that Pete Campbell asked me to call. Here's my cell number, if Ms. Small wants to call me before I call at three: 555-5555. Thanks, Art.

Speaking with a User
You are speaking face-to-face:

YOU: Laura, as you know, Ron has been a customer of mine for more than ten years. I know he's told you about our new widget, and—correct me if I'm mistaken—you are enthusiastic about features A, B, and C? Am I correct?

USER: Yes, I'm interested, but I'm not the one who writes the checks around here . . .

YOU: Oh, I understand that, Laura, which is why I'd like to get your help in convincing Ms. Dryer to make the purchase. Let me ask you this, how would *you* sell the widget to her? What features and functions are most important to you? What will persuade her that this is a great value and a wise decision? I think you're ready to step up to this widget, and you know I want to sell it to you. So let's help each other out.

Speaking with a Buyer

YOU: I know Ed Smith has spoken to you about the widget, Ms. Dryer, so I'm confident you understand just what it offers, particularly in three critical areas: efficient and economical use of materials, speed, and the benefit of our exclusive service guarantee. I don't want to take time covering ground you're familiar with, so perhaps you can help me out. Is there anything about these three critical areas you need to discuss further with me?

BUYER: No. But the fact is that the capital cost of the machinery is steep.

YOU: We both know that more important than cost is value. I know that there are cheaper widgets on the market. We ourselves offer two models at lower initial cost. However, for your needs—and based on what Ed has laid out to me—this model is by far your best value, especially with its low materials usage. No other widget can match that. You've seen the figures, and when we service the unit quarterly, each quarter we will give you a performance report. You'll see the figures for yourself, and so will the divisional head, if you want to share it with him. In fact, if it will help you make the decision, I can supply you with some sample usage reports from other customers. I want to give you whatever you need to make this decision—to make this happen.

Speaking with a Champion

YOU: Sarah, I feel that I'm awfully close to making this sale and delivering to you folks the right equipment you need. At this point, I think I need to nail down the value proposition, justifying what I know is a substantial initial cost. Is there anything in addition to low materials usage and speed of production that I can introduce to get the sale over the hump?

CHAMPION: We are a green company. I know your sales literature presents the energy costs quite well, but putting those figures in a nutshell might be just what we need to get Paula Dryer to pull the trigger.

YOU: Can I ask a favor? Would you go with me to see her this afternoon?

GET REFERRALS

There are three broad types of contacts in sales. Let's call them:

1. Cold
2. Warm
3. Hot
4. Hottest

A *cold contact*, or *cold call*, is an email (individual direct message, never spam!), phone call, or face-to-face encounter with a prospect to whom you are essentially unknown. A cold call should never be a random shot in the dark—"Gee, maybe this guy is interested in buying a widget today"—but should be the result of at least some research; however, the contact is made without a prior "pre-approach" exchange. Contrary to popular mythology, cold calls aren't particularly difficult to make. You just make them. The *rejection* most cold calls receive, however, may become difficult—or at least very discouraging—to accept. Also, while they save the time and energy required to "warm up" your calls via networking, cold calls actually burn up time, since such a low percentage of them produce sales.

A *warm contact* is a call that follows some lead, typically a referral from a current customer or another person in your network.

A *hot contact* also follows a lead, but not a mere referral. In the hot contact, a current customer or another person in your network has directly recommended you and your merchandise to the prospect.

The *hottest contact* comes when a prospect calls *you*, announcing that she is in the market for what you are selling.

Depending on what you are selling, your prospecting will consist of a mix of these four types of contacts. Always work from hottest to coolest. Prospect the most promising customers first. Invest your time in them initially, then devote a segment of your day to maintaining and expanding your network. When you have satisfied these two priorities, try some cold calls.

Work Your Established Customers

As we've said earlier, your best prospect is your current customer. Always begin with her. If she tells you no, that she's not in the market right now, ask her if she knows somebody who is. One of the most gratifying surprises humanity has to offer is an eagerness to help—to help you and to help someone else. We all like to connect people to other people. A high percentage of your current customers will at the very least *try* to furnish you with leads. The core of your prospecting network is made up of your current customers. Start there. Follow their leads first.

Always remember: You may be selling cars or shoes or houses, but your core business is creating satisfaction. You don't build a business with sales. You build it with satisfied customers, who are the sources of more customers and further sales.

Work Your Network

Your network consists of current customers and potentially just about everyone else you know in your business field. This includes your vendors, service consultants—such as attorneys and accountants—and anyone you can think of who comes into contact with people you view as potential customers.

If you think of your network as a bunch of people you can pester for sales referrals, you won't ever build much of a network. Take a lesson from the websites of companies you most admire. The best of them don't *try* to sell. They *offer*. Mostly, they offer information of value to those who visit the website. For example, the website of a software company specializing in antivirus products offers an authoritative forum on malware and other computing hazards, while the website of a popular discount travel agency offers "exclusive" travel tips for an array of locations. Build a network by offering useful information and insight and by offering your help. Whenever you encounter information you think a member or members of your network will find useful, send it to them. When you encounter a person you think one of your network members should meet, make the introduction. Out of every twenty contacts you make with a network member, nineteen should be offers of information, introduction, or other items of value; only one should be a request for an introduction or referral.

EXAMPLES

Email to a Network Member, Offering Information

Joe:

Thought you would want to see the attached review of the top new color laser printers. You mentioned the other day that the folks in your office were in the market. These are really thorough reviews, which I think you'll find helpful.

Best,
Jane

Email to a Network Member, Asking for a Referral

Joe:

I just read in *Trade Journal* that XYZ Corporation is expanding its product line to include B2C as well as B2B. I'd really like the opportunity to present our B2C marketing packages to them, but I don't have a direct contact there. You do business with XYZ. Can you refer me to a decision maker there—and perhaps make an introduction? I know we can do a lot of good for them as they make their expansion, and I appreciate any help you can give me.

Best,
Jane

COLD CONTACTS

Remember, a *cold contact*, or *cold call*, is an email (direct message, not spam!), phone call, or face-to-face encounter with a prospect to whom you are essentially unknown. Random calling is a waste of time. Research likely prospects first.

Emails

Just because you are a stranger, don't come on like one. Do your homework. Find out what's going on in your industry and your community. Begin by defining some common ground.

Dear Ed Brown:

Just saw the announcement in *News Notes* that you've been promoted to systems manager. I don't know you personally, but I know your firm as one that doesn't promote the undeserving. Congratulations!

I would like to help you hit the ground running by inviting myself over to hear directly from you how I might assist you with the special logistics needs of your company. We offer modular logistical systems designed to fit you and your needs. We can deliver the benefits of custom-coded software with the instant turnaround and economy of software off the shelf. I hope you will take my call early next week when I ask for an appointment with you. In the meantime, why don't you log onto our website at www.abc.xyz?

Sarah Marx
smarx@abc.xyz
555.555.5555 x555

Dear Jan Wren:

I just read in today's *Personal Service Newsletter* that your firm is expanding by bringing your special brand of personal shopping into our region.

Welcome!

I'd like to help by offering my brain to pick. I've been selling in this area for ten years now, and I know the community well. Obviously, you folks have done your homework, but my perspective is here for the sharing.

I am sales director of a small, locally based custom-container maker. We do the kind of "message" packaging that, I'm sure, your customers will appreciate and respond to. I've attached to this email a PDF of our latest catalog. Please look it over. I'll call you next week to discuss our offerings and our pricing. If you can't wait to talk, give me a ring on my direct line, 555-555-0000, or send an email.

Again, congratulations—and welcome to our world!

Cordially,
Frank Koopersmith
Sales Director

Dear Pat Backus:

I'm writing precisely because I don't know you, you don't know me, and we've never done business with each other.

Where have you been?

We've been supplying local express delivery service to this area (please see attached map) since 1985. Nobody's faster, and nobody knows the territory better. Within our operating region, we guarantee fully bonded pickup and delivery within four hours—max.

Our couriers are all uniformed professionals. They project the quality image you demand and your customers expect. Will you let me send one to you to deliver our rate sheet and talk to you about our system? Just hit reply and tell me when we should come calling. We already have your address. As I said, we *know* the territory.

Regards,
Ben Aller
Owner

Phone Calls

Cold calls are long shots under the best of circumstances. You can significantly improve your odds of success by deliberately moving the goalpost closer to you. Instead of deciding that making a sale is the objective of the call, try something more feasible, such as just *setting up* a sales call. Here is an example:

> ADMINISTRATIVE ASSISTANT: Hello, Ms. Smith's office. This is Jan.
>
> YOU: Good morning, Jan. I'm Paul Saunders from ABC Company. Could you connect me, please, with the person in charge of equipment purchase?
>
> ADMINISTRATIVE ASSISTANT: That would be Jay Mann. I'll connect you.
>
> YOU: Thank you, Jan.
>
> JAY MANN: Jay Mann . . .
>
> YOU: Good morning, Mr. Mann. I'm Paul Saunders from ABC Company. I'd like to ask you a question, if I might. Do you currently use widgets?
>
> JAY MANN: We do.
>
> YOU: Are you familiar with our New Technology widget?
>
> JAY MANN: No.
>
> YOU: Well, let me ask you another question. Is your weekly volume greater than a thousand units?
>
> JAY MANN: Yes, it is.
>
> YOU: Then you will want to know about our New Technology widget, which is specifically designed for high-volume production at the lowest possible cost. Might I have your permission to send one of our representatives to your location with a demonstration unit?

Another tactic to increase the odds of your having a productive cold call is the research call. People naturally resist sales calls. The research call, however, makes no attempt to sell anything.

> YOU: Is this Pam Johnson?
>
> PAM JOHNSON: It is.

YOU: My name is Paul Saunders, and I'm calling from ABC Company to ask you a few things about your widget needs. Can you take just a moment to help me by answering some questions?

PAM JOHNSON: Okay.

YOU: Fantastic. Thanks. Do you currently use a widget?

PAM JOHNSON: No, we don't.

YOU: Please tell me why not.

PAM JOHNSON: We order our materials from out of house.

YOU: I see. A lot of companies do, of course, but are you aware that using a widget can increase your revenue an average of 15 percent on an annual basis?

PAM JOHNSON: Really?

YOU: Let me explain.

[After laying out the key points, continue:]

Would you like to learn more about our High Performance line of widgets, including costs and leasing options?

PAM JOHNSON: Yes. I'd like to investigate.

YOU: Let me set up a visit . . .

WARM CONTACTS

A *warm contact* is a call that follows some lead, typically a referral from a current customer or another person in your network. The ability to mention the name of someone in your prospect's network, to demonstrate that you and the prospect are not *total* strangers, but that you share an acquaintance or a colleague, is very powerful. It may not actually create trust, but it makes trust possible. It increases the perceived value of what you are about to say. Always lead with the connection.

Email

After securing a referral, follow up quickly with an email addressed directly to your contact. Always include a cc to the person in your network who made the referral.

Dear Joyce Otis:

I was talking yesterday with my client and (as it turns out) our mutual friend, Mo Azad, at DEF, about his temporary staffing needs. I've always admired how Mo is such an effective manager, in part because he never confuses standing still with stability. He recognizes that staff must expand and contract with the changing demands of business. But he also realizes that finding good *temporary* staff can easily turn out to be a full-time job for a manager. Ultimately, what he does best is run his department—and so he has for the past two years let my company, ABC Temps, handle his short-term staffing needs.

Well, before I left his office yesterday, our conversation turned to you. Mo tells me that you are looking to ramp up a major project and will need substantial short-term staff. Of course, if finding *good* temporary staff is a full-time job, finding *great* temporary staff takes even longer—probably more time than you've got. At ABC, recruiting great staff is all we do.

Our business is finding and furnishing great temporary employees for your business.

I've attached a brief questionnaire to this email, which will give you the opportunity to tell us what your needs are. Fill it out, email it back, and I will connect with you right away. Or, if you prefer, pick up the phone and give me a call now, at 555-555-5555. Let me show you how we can help.

Cordially,
Ben Perry
Staffing Consultant

The biggest benefit a referral gives you is the opportunity to keep your solicitation out of the spam folder.

Dear Mary Boone:

My client—and our mutual friend—John Klein tells me you need a vacation. Actually, what he *really* said was that you've earned a vacation.

As John knows, you *earn* your vacation—which should be time off from work, carefree and relaxing. It should not be just another chore: juggling reservations, calculating prices, fighting crowds, and scheduling months in advance. Certainly, taking a break shouldn't be harder work than the job you do the rest of the year, and getting to your destination shouldn't be as tough as your morning commute. What's even worse is having to elbow through a mob of fellow vacationers once you've arrived. Who needs more competition when you're *off* the clock?

John and my many other clients have discovered the benefits of a vacation that's easy, always available, relaxing, and so private that, in fact, *it's all yours and yours alone*. It's all about owning beautiful lakeside or other wooded property only a few hours away from home but a whole world away from the daily grind.

If you think this is something only the 1 percent can afford, think again. I'm betting it's well within your reach.

For twenty-five years, we at Vacation Properties Unlimited have been selling affordable properties—ranging from as little as one half acre to 20 acres, in the woods, on the lake, and near the beach—to hardworking folks like you who want relaxation and recreation that really is relaxing and fun. I've attached a full-color brochure to this message. I invite you to look it over, then give me a call at 555-555-5555 to discuss the many affordable options. The call is yours to make when you want to make it. I will *not* call you. You're too busy.

Cheers,
Ron Pearl
Sales Consultant

Phone Call

YOU: Good afternoon. My name is Mary Cody. Am I speaking with Frances Washington?

FRANCES WASHINGTON: Yes.

YOU: Ms. Washington, Ted Williams at HMR is a mutual friend. I have been his widget vendor for going on a year now, and he urged me to call you because he believes in our product and thought you'd like to hear about it, too. Do you have a moment?

FRANCES WASHINGTON: Just a moment.

YOU: Great. We at PlantCo manufacture widgets for a wide variety of companies like yours, including Acme, Smith, and, of course, HMR and others. I'd like to ask you a few quick questions to determine if our product line is right for you. It will take just a few minutes. According to Ted, you do use widgets. Is that correct?

FRANCES WASHINGTON: Yes it is.

YOU: May I ask who supplies you?

FRANCES WASHINGTON: A&R, mostly.

YOU: And are you satisfied with their quality and price? Or, let me put it this way, would you be interested in hearing what I have to offer?

FRANCES WASHINGTON: Honestly, I haven't given it all that much thought. Go ahead and tell me something about what you have.

YOU: Every widget in our line is unique and highly cost-effective. The top benefits include flexibility, scalability, and value. Our per-use cost is on average 10 percent below that of the competition. As users like Ted can tell you, that number is real and, of course, significant. We also service what we sell—on-site. I bet you don't have this benefit with A&R.

FRANCES WASHINGTON: No, we don't.

YOU: Let me email you a PDF of our full brochure. You can order directly from it or give me a call at 555-555-5555 (my number is on the brochure) and I'll walk you through it and answer any questions.

FRANCES WASHINGTON: Yes. And please say hello to Ted for me.

YOU: You know I will.

HOT CONTACTS

Like a warm contact, a *hot contact* follows a lead, but one that is more than a referral. In the hot contact, a current customer or another person in your network has directly recommended you and your merchandise to the prospect.

Email

Dear Jane Morris:

Your friend and mine, Pam Kline, just called to say she talked to you about me. Well, the conversation was really about your career, and how you're looking to reach the proverbial "next level." That's when, as I understand it, Pam told you about my firm, Opportunities Unlimited.

So let me introduce myself and tell you what we're about. I'm John Shafer, and I run Opportunities Unlimited, a company that asks you to answer six questions, not for us, but for yourself:

1. Do you have all the money you need to do everything you want?
2. Do you have all the money you need to get your kids a great education?
3. Do you have all the money you need to build a secure future for your family?
4. Do you have all the money you need to simply pay the bills?
5. Are you getting paid what you deserve for the job you do?
6. Do you have the job you deserve?

You know the answers, and if they're what I think they are, you *will* want to talk to me. The name of the company is the best introduction to what we do. Opportunities Unlimited will give you the keys you need to unlock your potential and work productively toward everything you deserve. Our program guides you through three of the biggest, most rewarding, and most exciting steps you've ever taken or will ever take:

First: We guide you through our unique Career Analyzer, a series of diagnostic evaluations you do yourself and in the privacy of your home. As revealing as they are fascinating, these tests will help you and our staff of experts determine just where your next career move should take you.

Second: We guide you through our special Reality Checker, a do-it-yourself kit that will enable you to determine just how much money you need *now* and to attain your *future goals*.

Third: We work with you to plan your campaign strategy to get you what you need, what you want, and what you deserve.

I have one more question. It's just one word: *Interested?*

If your answer is yes, I invite you to follow Pam's advice and give me a call at 555-555-5555. I'd love to work together with you.

Sincerely,
John Shafer

Phone Call

YOU: Is this Pat Moreland?

PAT MORELAND: Yes.

YOU: Mr. Moreland, it turns out we have a mutual friend, who is also one of my clients—Pam Kline. I just got off the phone with her. She gave me your number, said the two of you had just talked, and she urged me to call you. This is John Shafer, and I run Opportunities Unlimited, a company that—well, what we do is give you the keys you need to unlock your potential and work productively toward everything you deserve. Pam tells me that you are doing great work for BCD Corp., but that your upward mobility is pretty limited there. Do I understand the situation?

PAT MORELAND: Well, actually, yes. That's what we were talking about, and Pam did mention you and did suggest I call.

YOU: Well, while we're on the line together now, is this a good time to talk?

PAT MORELAND: Sure, sure it is.

YOU: Great. Over the past eight years, Mr. Moreland—may I call you Pat?

PAT MORELAND: Of course, please do.

YOU: Pat, over the past eight years, Opportunities Unlimited has offered more than twelve hundred clients a program we've formulated to guide you through three of the biggest, most rewarding, and most exciting steps you've ever taken or will ever take. We begin by taking you through our unique Career Analyzer, which is a series of diagnostic evaluations you do yourself and in the privacy of your home. You will find the Analyzer fascinating as well as challenging. The results will help

you and our staff of experts determine just where your next career move
should take you. But the *very next* move after the Career Analyzer will
be to our special Reality Checker, a self-directed worksheet that will enable you to determine just how much money you need *now* and to attain your *future goals*. Finally, we take the Analyzer and Reality Checker
results and work with you, one-on-one, to plan your campaign strategy
to get you what you need, what you want, and what you deserve.

That's it in a nutshell. What questions of yours can I answer?

PAT MORELAND: What's it all cost?

YOU: The onetime fee is $XXX. There are no extras or add-ons. And the
fee includes, beyond the Career Analyzer, Reality Checker, and planning session, a full year of follow-up consultation service. We can talk
you through specific situations, steps, and plans as they arise.

PAT MORELAND: Do you have any literature on the program—not that
your pitch wasn't great . . .

YOU: Pat, I understand. Give me your email address, and I will send a
brochure right out to you. Look it over, and I'm confident I'll be hearing back from you. In the meantime, this has been a pleasure.

HOTTEST CONTACTS

The *hottest contact* comes when a prospect calls you, announcing that she is
in the market for what you are selling. Everything you say should be directed
toward facilitating what the customer's call signals, namely closing the sale.

EXAMPLE

Responding to the Hottest Contact

CALLER: I'm looking for car insurance.

YOU: I can help you. As an independent full-service automobile insurance
agency, we will get you not only the lowest-priced auto insurance, but
see to it that you get just the coverage that you need—no more and no
less. Let me ask you some questions. [*Proceed immediately to the full*

application. Complete it. The objective in closing this sale is not only to get the information required to make the sale, but to ensure that the prospect invests his time with you. This gives the prospect a stake in your offering and significantly increases the odds of your successfully closing the sale. Having completed the application, continue:]

YOU: Okay. We've completed the application. I would like to make some recommendations for increasing the coverage above the state-required minimums. Auto insurance isn't just about obeying the law, it's about protecting yourself and your family. May I make some suggestions?

CALLER: Sure, but I don't want to spend money on insurance I don't need.

YOU: Well, I'm not here just to sell you an insurance policy. I'm here to make you a client—over the long term. I'm here to see that you are satisfied. So, no, I don't want to sell you anything you don't need. But I do know the industry, I do know the courts, I do know the level of liability lawyers go gunning for, and I certainly know this community. My recommendations are based on my experience.

CALLER: Okay.

YOU: *[Present your recommendation package. Then close the sale.]* So, here are your total coverages and your monthly premium. If you give me a credit card number now for the first month's premium, your coverage begins immediately. Of course, paperwork will follow in the mail. You can review the policy, and if you have any questions, please call. Shall we get your policy into force right now, then?

WORDS AND PHRASES TO USE

Act	Create
Advise	Deal direct
Always available	Deliver satisfaction
Assist	Direct
Benefit	Discerning
Best price	Exciting news
Committed to you	Expect more
Confident	Extra

Help me
Here to serve you
High value
Immediate
Interesting news
Let us help
Listen to you
Make a connection/
    an introduction
Opportunity
Personal service
Savvy
Smart
Solution

Something you can use
Special value
Start-to-finish
Successful
Unique opportunity
Valuable
We can help
We care
We listen
We're here to help
Welcome
What do you need?
You can talk to us

WORDS AND PHRASES TO AVOID

Absolutely must
Don't drop the ball
Drop everything
I hate to do this to you
I know this is the last thing you
    want to do, but
I've got to ask you
Last chance

Matter of life or death
Need from you
No choice
Sorry to bother you
Urgent
Want from you
You have to

CHAPTER 3

Speak Value

It's no secret that selling and salespeople get a bad rap in our society. The pop-culture sales stereotypes range from *disreputable* to *loser*. Just think of "Professor" Harold Hill in *The Music Man*, Willy Loman in *Death of a Salesman*, or any of the real estate–selling swindlers in David Mamet's great *Glengarry Glen Ross*. Yet the truth is that selling is at the very core of civilization. Its basis is the exchange of values: *You want something of value to you; I give it to you in exchange for something of value to me.* Nothing could be more basic or more essential or more important. To be a salesperson is to be engaged in the profession of communicating value for the purpose of receiving value. Fail to deliver fair value for the value you receive, and you are the ultimate "disreputable" salesperson: a thief. Fail to receive fair value for the value you deliver, and you are a "loser": a *Death of a Salesman* failure. Fail to clearly and persuasively communicate the relevant issues of value, of offering and exchange, and your prospects will *assume* you are either "disreputable" or a "loser." Succeed in communicating value, however, and you become a master practitioner of a noble, civilization-building profession. This chapter is about speaking value to prospects and customers.

CREATE A VALUE STATEMENT

To begin with, stop trying to sell a product or a service. Start selling value instead. To do this, you will need a value statement, which is also called a *direct value statement*. This statement should always embody three elements:

1. It should state the reason for your firm's existence.
2. It should state why you have chosen to sell your firm's products or services.
3. It should convey these statements clearly, affirmatively, and—in a word—*directly*.

At first glance, you might think that the idea of the direct value statement is not really "direct" at all because it does not *directly* state what product or service you are selling. The fact is that, usually, what you are selling is self-evident: insurance, automobiles, shoes. You don't need to waste time or insult your prospect's intelligence by stating what he already knows. Even worse, you don't want to reinforce or ratify what your prospect most likely *assumes*, which is something like *This guy is a salesman. All he cares about is selling me a car.* That is, your prospect assumes you are totally self-interested or, more precisely, that your interest in him, the prospect, depends entirely on what *he* can do for *you*. Your prospect may even assume, at some level, that the salesperson's gain will necessarily be his—the customer's—loss. In truth, a successful, satisfying sale is a win for both salesperson and customer. Both gain value, so that both are richer for the exchange, even though the one parts with merchandise and the other parts with cash. But this is not how most prospective customers see the salesperson-customer relationship. To get them to see it this way, you need an effective value statement.

Instead of announcing what you have to sell—which is really a statement of what you want the prospect to buy—create a value statement that:

1. Tells the prospect what your organization is, does, and stands for.
2. Tells the prospect what you do and how you do it *for your customers*.
3. Tells the prospect what value—what benefits—you deliver.

4. Shows your prospect the group of satisfied customers she will join if she chooses to do business with you.

In short, the value statement is not about the merchandise. It is about the prospective customer. It does not describe the *attributes* or *features* of the merchandise. It defines the *benefit* that owning the merchandise will confer on the customer.

A few years ago, a well-known express delivery service used this tagline in much of its advertising: "When it absolutely, positively has to get there on time." This is a slogan founded on a direct value statement. Instead of describing the main *feature* of the service being sold—namely, overnight delivery—the line sells the value (the *benefit* to the customer) of reliability (actually, the value of the certainty of *absolute* reliability), which is confidence, peace of mind, and enhancement of reputation (the person who ships via an absolutely reliable express company earns himself a reputation for absolute reliability). If you were a salesperson for this company, your value statement might be something like "We help customers to feel confident and secure in their reputation for absolute reliability by providing overnight delivery of goods on time, every time. I get great personal and professional satisfaction from producing this high level of satisfaction for my customers, making them feel great and enhancing their reputation among their colleagues and clients. That's why I'm in this business." Having delivered this value statement—a statement of *benefits*—you might continue by delivering a description of *features*, explaining the actual process by which your company gets the shipment to its destination overnight and on time, every time.

More recently, a maker of luxury SUVs has been advertising its product with a television commercial that shows a seven-person family—dad, mom, kids (the point is that the vehicle "comfortably" seats seven)—backing out of the driveway of a lovely suburban house. Cut to a shot of a neighborhood child pushing his teddy bear down the sidewalk in a toy car. As the family's SUV backs down the driveway, the child and his toy car enter the intersection of the driveway and the sidewalk. If this were an ordinary SUV, the child would be in the driver's blind spot and in imminent danger of being hit. But this is no ordinary SUV. It not only is equipped with a rearview video camera, it also has a system that activates the brakes when an object is sensed behind the vehicle. Tragedy is averted. Momentary concern and instant relief are evident on the faces of family members riding in the SUV.

The *feature* being sold in this commercial is safety technology—specifically, a rearview video camera and an automatic braking system. These are attributes of the vehicle. The *benefit* that is promoted relates not to the car, but to the family. It is nothing less than their continued well-being, security, peace of mind, preservation of conscience, and freedom from liability. The *benefit* this particular SUV offers is protecting everyone's life—that of the passing child (literally) and the life of the SUV family, which could have been emotionally shattered and financially ruined by a tragic accident. A value statement for this product might be something of this sort: "We bring families together and protect them from harm in an SUV that also offers comfort while projecting the owner's impeccable good taste. I am passionate about selling a reliable, beautiful vehicle that provides safety and peace of mind." Again, once this direct value proposition is stated, you might transition from the benefits to the features—just how the rearview camera works and how the system triggers application of the brake.

Sample Value Statements

Here are some direct value statements:

We partner with physicians to improve relations with their patients and thereby produce improved outcomes. We do this through our cost-effective physician sensitivity DVD series. I have seen how building a more satisfying relationship between doctor and patient creates better outcomes for patients and deeper professional satisfaction for physicians. That is why I'm excited to offer this product.

We assist e-commerce providers to increase their online visibility and sales. We do this by customizing free online informational products that draw customers to our clients' websites. Helping clients stand out from the online crowd is a challenge, but the dramatic increase in revenue my clients experience is always a thrill to see.

We help our clients in the home furnishing industry get their products to market faster, which not only gains them a competitive edge, but significantly reduces warehousing costs. Assisting hardworking men and women in streamlining their business processes is what I'm all about. I never get tired of collaborating on success.

We bring luxury to the kitchen. When our customers use our line of cutlery, they have the unique thrill of working with the finest instruments on the planet—and that moves them to create cuisine to match. I'm convinced that cooking should be a pleasure, and that meals prepared using the best and most beautiful implements are the more delicious for it.

WORDS AND PHRASES TO USE

Be confident	Facilitate
Best	Feel great about
Build satisfaction	Increase revenues
Cost-effective	Maximize
Create confidence/success/value	Passionate
Delight	Peace of mind
Empower	Set the standard
Enable	Top-quality
Enhance	Unmatched

WORDS AND PHRASES TO AVOID

Adequate	Low-cost
As good as it needs to be	Minimum
Bargain	Quick and dirty
Dirt cheap	Sell
Giveaway	

CREATE DISSATISFACTION

A builder, everyone knows, builds. But, very often, in order to build, a builder first has to knock down, to demolish whatever structure occupies the site slated for the new project. In the same way, while a salesperson's objective is to create customer satisfaction, very often she must first create dissatisfaction. If you want to sell widget B to a prospective customer who already owns widget A, it will be necessary either to persuade him that he needs at least two widgets or that he is actually dissatisfied (or *should* be dissatisfied) with widget A and can achieve satisfaction only by acquiring widget B.

EXAMPLE
Here is a prospecting email:

Do you suffer from parental paranoia? It's that nagging, guilty, worrisome feeling that you could be doing more to help your child excel in school and gain the edge he or she needs to get into the best college and embark on a truly rewarding career.

The last thing I want to do is drive you crazy, but I do want to disturb you, at least a little—a little that can mean a great deal to your child.

What's in your Family Digital Library? Do you even have a Family Digital Library? Your child needs a foundation of great books to give him or her an advantage beyond what even the best classrooms offer. My company can help you give your child that competitive cultural edge.

We're Educational Advice Associates, an organization of top-level educators and seasoned teachers who have given a lifetime of thought to just what books children need to read at each grade level to give them the competitive cultural edge. Now, this is an ever-evolving requirement, and no single guidebook can hope to give you all the answers. So we offer *Educational Advisor Online*, sent to you monthly to bring you and your child:

Suggested and "Must Have" additions to your Family Digital Library.
Updates on websites, blogs, magazines, and television shows of value to your child.
Step-by-step guidance on building a Family Digital Library.
Hot issues in education that will have impact on you and your child.

And there is more. We offer exclusive direct online links to the great books we recommend, so that you can download them instantly to your computer, tablet, smartphone, or e-reader. Many of these books are absolutely free. The rest are offered to you at a substantial subscriber discount.

Make your life and that of your children better. Give yourself the satisfaction and peace of mind that come with the knowledge that you are giving your children the learning equipment he or she needs for today—for tomorrow—and for all the school days to come.

The Questions to Ask

Change begins when people question the way things are. "Do we have to be ruled by King George III? No? Then why not declare independence and start a revolution?" Create dissatisfaction by asking your prospect questions:

Does your insurance company give you all the value you need?

Does your insurance company give you the protection you need?

Does your insurance company give you the feeling of confidence and peace of mind you and your family deserve?

Are you paying too much for your car loan?

Are you paying too much at the grocery store?

Is your child getting the best education?

Do you own the highest definition flat screen ever made?

Could you be eating healthier?

Are you getting as much out of your life as you should?

Do you have all the retirement income you need?

Do you know how much retirement income you will need?

Are your gutters rusting away?

Do you have termites?

Are termites destroying your family's biggest investment?

Is your online reputation in danger?

Is somebody stealing your identity?

Are you getting too old too fast?

Could you be feeling better than you do?

Are you satisfied with your outdoor grill?

Are you getting enough fun out of life?

Is your house making you sick?

Is the water you drink safe?

Is your necktie telling people you are not to be trusted?

Are you getting the best mileage possible out of your current car?

You can even ask questions that invite the prospect to imagine dissatisfaction:

Will you ever find an insurance company that will give you all the value you need?

Will you end up paying too much for your next car loan?

Will your child's school fail to give her the education she really needs?

Will you ever buy the highest definition flat screen ever made?

Will you discover that you don't have enough money for retirement after all?

Will your health insurance plan be there when you really need it?

Will your house be attacked by termites?

Will you be as happy with your car in ten years as you are today?

Will someone steal your identity?

If you ever doubt the power of questioning satisfaction to create dissatisfaction and close the sale, turn the pages of your history book to 1980, when presidential candidate Ronald Reagan asked voters: *Are you better off today than you were four years ago?* Reagan won the election, of course, carrying 44 out of 50 states and winning 489 electoral votes to just 49 for Jimmy Carter (six states and Washington, DC).

COMMUNICATE FEATURES, SELL BENEFITS

Every item of merchandise, whether it is a product or a service, has features and offers benefits. Features are descriptive attributes of the product or service, such as built-in GPS, seven-speed transmission, twenty-inch alloy wheels. Benefits are what the product or service will do for the customer.

They are the value offered. They are the changes—the improvements—that purchasing the merchandise will bring to the customer's life: "With its built-in GPS, you'll always know where you're going. With a seven-speed transmission, you'll get there fast. And your arrival on twenty-inch alloy wheels *will* get you noticed."

Telephone Sales Call

Here is a telephone sales call that creates dissatisfaction, communicates features, and sells benefits:

> YOU: Good morning, <prospect name>. I'm <your name> with <your company>. We manufacture <products> for many companies like yours, including <list two or three well-known customers>. May I ask you a question?
>
> PROSPECT: All right.
>
> YOU: Do you currently use <type of product>?
>
> PROSPECT: We do.
>
> YOU: Are you satisfied with the value your current suppliers deliver?
>
> PROSPECT: Do you mean price?
>
> YOU: Price, yes, but, more important, the *value*: Are you getting your money's worth?
>
> PROSPECT: Always looking for a better deal . . .
>
> YOU: Then let me tell you what we offer. Our <product> is unique and highly cost-effective. It provides the features most sought-after by companies like yours: <list features>. But everybody makes a <product> with decent features. What we offer is a degree of quality and service that will give you peace of mind, confidence, and the assurance that when you tell a customer you will deliver the best, you will do so with the knowledge that your equipment is the best and is backed by 24/7 on-site service. *That* is something no other company offers as a standard feature.
>
> PROSPECT: What price range are we talking about?
>
> YOU: Inclusive of setup and two years of on-site service, our models range from $XXXX to $XXXX.

PROSPECT: Tell me more about the service contract . . .

YOU: [*Specify contract features, then end with benefits:*] What this means is that, no matter what happens, even in the worst case, your down-time will never be more than X hours. Can you put a price tag on the benefit of absolute reliability? We won't give you excuses, so you won't have to pass excuses on to your customers. Now, we could not provide 24/7 service if our product was unreliable. In fact, we don't expect anything to go wrong—but we are there for you if it does. You're not just buying a machine. You're buying performance. You're buying integrity.

WORDS AND PHRASES TO USE

24/7

A phone call away

Around the clock

Assurance

Call our product specialists

Consultation

Continuing assistance

Dependable

Enduring commitment

Exclusive access to our product specialists

Integrity

It's never *your* problem. It's *our* problem.

Just ask

Just the way you like/need/want it

Peace of mind

Personal attention

We deliver integrity/quality/value; you pass it on to your customers

We'll do it all for you

WORDS AND PHRASES TO AVOID

As soon as we can get to it

Automated call center

Force majeure

Hit or miss

I think you'll be satisfied

I've never heard that complaint before

Limited warranty

Put you on the service queue

Subject to availability

That is unlikely

That never happens

We do the best we can

We get very few complaints

You can't beat the price

WORDS AND PHRASES THAT PROMISE SOLUTIONS

WORDS AND PHRASES TO USE

A perfect alternative

All you will ever need

An attractive solution to an ugly problem

Best value

Dream come true

Exclusive to you

Expert advice/answers/solutions

Flexible

Ideal for your application

Imagine never having to think about <problem> again

It is the best-practice solution

It's just what you need

Just the right amount

Perfect solution

The answer you've been looking for

You've found what you've been looking for

WORDS AND PHRASES TO AVOID

Can't

Can't expect miracles

Limit to what can be done

Must not

No choice

Not in our best interest

Not worth it to us

This is the best we can do

You are asking for the impossible

WORDS AND PHRASES THAT PROMISE SATISFACTION

WORDS AND PHRASES TO USE

A sure bet

All your professional needs met

Always in stock

Customized service

Exceed your expectations

Gives you the same edge as the pros

Goes the distance

Guaranteed

Impressive results

Lasts forever

Leave it to us

Many included extras

Nothing else to buy—ever

Relax

Takes you to the next level

We produce results

We stake our reputation on your
    complete satisfaction

When you need an expert

You are always in the loop

You are in good hands

You are the boss

You call the shots

WORDS AND PHRASES TO AVOID

Against our policy

As is

Better than nothing

I can explain

It's not our fault

Our other customers are
    satisfied

Take a chance

This is what you ordered

This works for everyone else

Too late

We need to make a living, too

Well, it is one size fits all

You should be satisfied

CHAPTER 4

Sing AIDA

I can offer no silver-bullet formula for making sales and creating satisfied customers, because no single formula can control all four of the variables involved in a sales situation:

1. The *actual* character of the salesperson and how the prospect *perceives* that character.
2. The skill of the salesperson.
3. The needs and desires of the prospect.
4. The intrinsic desirability—quality and value—of the merchandise on offer.

Many authorities on salesmanship will tell you that you do not sell a *product*, you sell *yourself*. As you saw in Chapter 1, there is truth in this, and a big part of selling is creating and conveying confidence in yourself. However, you cannot ignore the actual merchandise on offer. Certainly, your prospect will not ignore it. Unless what you sell is offered at a ridiculously low price, it is always easier to sell merchandise of obvious value than it is to sell junk. It feels better, too.

So now you know what I cannot do. I cannot furnish a sovereign formula for sales, because I cannot tell you how to control the main variables in the selling situation. I can, however, suggest a method for influencing those variables, coaxing them to go your way. Good sales communication—by email, web page copy, phone call, or face-to-face encounter—can build a positive image of the salesperson's character as well as the integrity of the company she represents. It can also enhance the skill of the seller, and not least of all, it can do wonders to create the necessary desire in the prospect.

NEW LIFE FOR AN OLD FORMULA

There is no hard-and-fast outline for effective sales communication, but over the years—centuries, really—sales professionals have created a slew of templates. Most have deservedly fallen into disuse, but at least one is both basic and flexible enough not only to have survived, but to be truly useful and effective. Opera lovers will recognize it as the title of a Verdi masterpiece, but veteran sales professionals revere it as a valuable acronym. AIDA stands for Attention, Interest, Desire, Action. It is a compact guide to making a sale.

A: First, capture the prospect's *Attention.* Often, this may be done by delivering your *direct value statement,* as discussed in Chapter 3. Whatever attention-getting statement you use, make it short, and make it provocative. An alternative to a declarative value statement is asking a provocative question. The advantage of this approach is that a question automatically elicits attention, since it calls for an interactive response—*yes, no,* and so on. Questions such as the following all command attention:

"Could you use free cash right now?"
"Is your job about to disappear?"
"Are you preparing your child for success?"
"Do you deserve a promotion?"
"Does your health insurance provide state-of-the-art coverage?"
"Do you have what it takes to be a CEO?"

I: Of course, you can also attract attention with a shout, a sharp clap of the hands, or a rude noise made under your arm. The problem is that such attention—any attention, really—is short-lived. Attention by itself is not sufficient to make a sale; therefore, once you've gotten a prospect's attention, you have to develop it rapidly into *Interest*. This is best done by explaining—in the proverbial nutshell—your value proposition. The persuasive emphasis must be on the opportunity the proposed deal represents. This means shining a light not on the features of the merchandise on offer, but on the benefits—the beneficial, problem-solving, life-enhancing impact on the potential user or owner of the product or service.

D: As attention must be rapidly escalated to interest, so interest must quickly morph into *Desire*, if you expect to close the sale—that is, to move the prospect to action. Your objective in this phase of the sales communication is to put what you imagine is your prospect's desire into your own words. Express what he feels. Mirror his desire. Let him hear it and see it. Desire is a motivation that must first be stirred and then rendered urgent. Make the desire urgent by letting your prospect know that he is not alone. "Everybody will want to take advantage of this opportunity." Or: "You do not want to be shut out." Or: "A chance like this comes along maybe once every ten years."

A: The most basic lesson every Las Vegas gambler learns is *never leave money on the table*. Inexplicably, however, many otherwise talented and capable salespeople do just this. Having captured a prospect's attention, developed it into interest, and converted the interest to desire, they abruptly end the pitch, expecting the *prospect* to make the next move. Sometimes, the prospect does just that. Often, however, the exchange, promising though it has been, simply ends—the money left on the table. The last letter of the AIDA acronym stands for *Action*, and it is what you must move your prospect to undertake. Tell her what to do next. Provide instructions that will prompt her to act as you want her to act. Sir Isaac Newton's First Law of Motion defines inertia in the physical world: *Every object continues in its state of rest, or of uniform motion in a straight line, unless compelled to change that state by external forces acted upon it*. This pretty well describes human motivation as well. The first three stages of the AIDA formula have been aimed at preparing the prospect to overcome inertia. The fourth stage provides the "external force" necessary to do that, to get the prospect to deviate from his straight line or get him moving in the first place. All sales communication—

every pitch—must culminate in a call to action. Without it, you are abandoning your prospect, hoping—just hoping—that he will make the transition from the realm of words (attention and interest) and emotion (desire) to action (parting with money) all on his own. The gentlest push is more effective than the most fervent hope, but you can put a little muscle behind the shove by introducing a special offer or other incentive at the final A.

GET ATTENTION

Here are some lines for the first A, designed to get a prospect's attention. They can be applied to any medium of contact: letter, email, web copy, phone solicitation, even a face-to-face encounter.

> Do you share your chair with somebody else? How about your pens and pencils? But you say you share *your computer*?
>
> Can you afford to be number two, three, four, or more in line to get access to the latest industry news?
>
> When it comes to <product or service>, only the best will do. Well, now you have a clear choice. Introducing . . .
>
> We create opportunities for companies just like yours.
>
> There is a striking new approach to providing <service>, and we are the only company in the region that offers it.
>
> We bring the benefits of breakthrough innovation in <product or service> directly to you.
>
> We enable you to deliver the most advanced <service> to your customers at a competitive price.
>
> If you want to break ahead of the pack, you will want to hear about our new <product or service>.
>
> We are determined to make you successful in the <type of> business. Let me tell you how.

WORDS AND PHRASES TO USE

A breakthrough advance	A new experience/sensation/
A fresh approach	solution

Ahead of the crowd

Discovery

Dynamic

Everything you need/want

First time ever

It's finally your turn

Prepare to be satisfied

Scientific

Unexpected

Unique opportunity

Updated

Years ahead

WORDS AND PHRASES TO AVOID

Cheap! Cheap! Cheap!

I need to tell you something

I want to sell you something

I won't keep you long

Let me trouble you for a few
   minutes of your time

Please, listen to me

This may interest you

This won't take long

Trust me

GENERATE INTEREST

Moving from getting attention to creating interest requires presenting your product or service in some detail. For example:

We offer high-value vacation experiences for people who are not happy just following the crowd. Our destinations include <list>. We offer customized tours, if you want them, or we just get you there and leave you alone if that's what you prefer.

You know quality when it comes to making <product>. We know quality when it comes to creating the kind of corporate gifts that can forge a special bond with your customers. Our gift line conveys your unique identity while showing your customers just how much you care about them. If you want to build quality relationships, why not invest a few minutes at our website, xyz.xyz, to tour our latest selection? Everything you'll see there is fully customizable.

What we offer you is choice and control. It is true this makes our system seem a bit more complex than some others, but it is actually easy to learn, and learning to use it puts all the power of choice in your hands. Our software expands the possibilities. Try it, and you will experience the feeling of really being in charge.

The new alarm system has designed-in redundancy that gives you and your family an unprecedented level of security. It sends a signal to our monitoring station simultaneously with the police or the fire department, depending on the type of alarm. We immediately contact you, followed by a call to police or fire. If the alarm is false, we stop the responders before they roll. If you confirm the emergency or if we cannot reach you, we're already on the phone to the responders and we can tell them, instantly, that the alarm is real. Redundancy means total peace of mind, and we're the only vendor in this market that offers it to residential customers.

We are not your typical take-it-or-leave-it caterer. The service we offer is collaborative. *You* help us plan. *You* share your vision with us. *We* make it happen. There will be no surprises, and there will be no hidden or unexpected costs. We begin the planning process together, we invite you to monitor our implementation of the plan at every step, and in this way, we cater not just to your guests, but to your wishes, your imagination, your dreams.

This economy is tough on everyone, but not in the *same way* on everyone. That is why we design solutions expressly to satisfy your needs and suit your specifications. Let me ask you: What obstacles loom largest for you right now? Once I understand *your* situation from *your* perspective, I can present solutions that won't work for everybody, but *will* work for *you*.

WORDS AND PHRASES TO USE

Best practices

Conveys quality in every detail—
    for example . . .

Gives you the competitive edge

Here's why it's so rare

Here's why it's such a good value

I can prove it

I can show you how to fix that

Imagine

It is easy to use

Let me show you how it works

Let me tell you how

No one else delivers this level of
quality and this level of price

Provides a lot of options

See for yourself

Shall we review the entire range of
options?

Smart

Taps into your creativity

This is an investment in your
future

Unlike any you have used before

We can create virtually any
design

We deliver profits for your
business, and I can show
you how

We stock a huge inventory

You should ask me to prove it

You will be amazed by what I'm
about to say

WORDS AND PHRASES TO AVOID

Barebones

Generic

It is what it is

No frills

Nothing to explain

Take it or leave it

Traditional

Vanilla

What more can I say?

You know the drill

You've seen this before

CREATE DESIRE

To move from interest to desire is to move from head to heart and from features to benefits. Don't be afraid to stir emotion. In fact, it is essential that you do just this.

Wouldn't it be a thrill to own—and use—a product like this?

Now you can know the feeling of owning the best <product> in the world.

Our system will solve your problems now and for years to come. There is no benefit greater than total peace of mind.

This degree of comfort was inconceivable until now. Think of how you will feel when you switch on the XYZ 900.

Incomparable aesthetics, individuality, and quality of materials and workmanship. What does that mean *to* you? What will that say *about* you?

No automobile is safer. And isn't that what you really want for your family?

They say that the quality of a craftsman's tools proclaim the quality of the craftsman. What do your tools proclaim about you? Could this be the time to step up to a set of ABC chisels?

Our quit-smoking program will not only help you save your life, it will make your life better. It will give you back your freedom and your pride. It will replace the stale taste of old smoke and dead nicotine with the fresh savor of victory won.

Take your finger and run it along every seam, every door edge on this vehicle. Feel the quality. Now open the door. Get in. *Drive* the quality.

This kind of jewelry is not for everyone. That is the rare, rare beauty and appeal of it. It marks you as one in precisely five million.

WORDS AND PHRASES TO USE

A taste like no other

An experience few have had

Buy this, and people will look at you in a new way

Feel the power

Feel the quality in the palm of your hand

Imagine the convenience

It *can* be yours

Know the pleasure of quality

Leaves you feeling refreshed *and* relaxed

Less fatigue, more fun

Our guarantee tells you you've made the right decision

Rare delight

Relaxing

Safe

Stop smoking now, stop smoking forever

Stop the pain—now

This is what control sounds like

Warning: You *will* be envied

We take the worry out of insurance

What a feeling!

What would it feel like . . .

You *can* have it all

You will use them with pride

WORDS AND PHRASES TO AVOID

Adequate

For better or worse

For the price

Good enough

I haven't received any complaints

I'm no expert

It is what it is

It's a <product>, what more is
there to say?

Meets minimum standards

No one has ever asked for *that*
before

That's something the
manufacturer doesn't tell us

Unavailable

We don't have that
information

Why would you want that?

ENABLE ACTION

The mechanics of closing the sale—provision of a means to actually place an order and pay for it—need to be in place, so that the final A need be little more than a set of easy-to-follow instructions, perhaps with some reiteration of the just-concluded D stage. If the customer must supply information or documentation to complete the purchase, be certain to include these instructions in the call to action.

Click on "ORDER NOW" to take advantage of this offer. We accept all major credit cards and PayPal.

Call 555-555-5555 to set up this exclusive service today. If you would like an exclusive Express Estimate, please be sure to have all room dimensions on hand when you call. If you prefer, we will come out to your location, do all the measuring for you, and give you your price on the spot. There is no additional charge for this complete concierge service. Call today, 555-555-5555.

Stop by any of our convenient locations to see the Super 100 and Super 200 in action. Our experts will answer any questions you may have. Our locations in your area are <list locations and addresses>, and we are open seven days a week, from 9 to 6. You don't want to miss this.

When you order, please be certain to have your physician's prescription in hand.

Our sales hotline is available 24/7 to serve you. Call 555-555-5555 or go to www.xyz.xyz. That's all it takes to experience the sublime satisfaction of owning the very best.

We live to serve. Please call us at 555-555-5555. One of our expert counselors will walk you through the decision and purchasing process. All your questions will be answered, and there are no obligations or charges for the call.

The Wonder Widget is available only with this Special Offer, which is being made for a limited time only. Don't miss out. Call 555-555-5555. We accept all major credit cards—and, remember, shipping is absolutely free.

Why suffer another day? Call 555-555-5555 or visit www.xyz.xyz right now. Associates are available 24/7 to answer your questions and process your order. But you must act now.

WORDS AND PHRASES TO USE

Act now

Come talk to us

Easy financing is available

Free trial

If not now, when?

Imagine using the Super 100 just three days from today

In no time at all

Leave it to us

Look forward to professional, friendly service—always

No obligation

See for yourself

Start feeling the difference today

Supplies are limited

Talk to us about our payment plans

We do all the heavy lifting

We make it easy for you

We pamper you

We won't put you on hold. We promise.

We've built our payment
    plans around *you*. Come
    talk to us.
What are you waiting for?

What can we do for you?
You risk nothing
You're a phone call away from
    complete satisfaction

WORDS AND PHRASES TO AVOID

As is
Find us at most popular outlets
Give it some thought
If the line is busy, keep trying

If your neighborhood store
    doesn't have it, keep on
    looking
Maybe you should consider us
Must
No guarantee

CHAPTER 5

Overcome Objections

Most sales calls and presentations elicit at least some objections: reasons not to buy. Objections are part of the sales process. Don't fear them, don't try to evade them, and never ignore them. Welcome them. They are signs of the prospect's interest in your offering—and that is much better than lack of interest and *way* better than your simply being shown the door. Even more important, each of the prospect's objections is an opportunity to deliver an answer that will create satisfaction and thereby make the sale.

An expressed objection is a gift from the prospect to you. Embrace it, open it, say thank you, then *use* it to close the sale. An unexpressed—or hidden—objection is a land mine that threatens to blow up the sale. If you don't know what is preventing the prospect from buying, you cannot know how to address, and perhaps solve, the problem. For this reason, never seek to avoid or to gloss over objections. Anticipate them, and probe for them. Listen *for* them, and listen *to* them. Don't interrupt the prospect, and resist the natural tendency to respond defensively. Discuss the objections, and endeavor to overcome them.

ANTICIPATE

Your best chance of converting objections into sales is to understand your merchandise and your customers so thoroughly that you can anticipate likely objections and counter them with responses you have already thought out and formulated. Study your product and services, and study those of your competitors. Talk to other sales professionals in your field, talk to your current customers, and talk to prospective customers. Understand the wants, the needs, and the concerns of all of these groups.

When you make a sales presentation, product benefits and features should be uppermost in your mind and in your pitch. Running a very close second to these, however, should be the objections you anticipate. If, after making your presentation, you make a sale, that's just great. If you meet with an objection, consider that only a little less positive a result. You can deal with an objection, and you have a fighting chance to overcome it. It is possible, however, that you will meet with neither acceptance nor stated objections, but silence or stall signals. These signals may be verbal, including such responses as:

> "I need to think about it."
> "Let me think about it."
> "I just don't know . . ."
> "I'm not sure . . ."
> "Certainly very interesting . . ."
> "Well, that *is* something to think about."
> "You've given me a lot to think about."
> "I don't think I'm ready to buy just yet."

Or they may be nonverbal, body language cues. For example:

Looking down or to the side—eyes directed anywhere except at you.
Arms crossed across chest.
Shuffling of feet.
If the prospect is sitting, movement of feet.
Backing away from you.

Turning away from you.
Hand brought to mouth.
Hand rubbing chin.
Hand rubbing forehead.
Hand rubbing back of neck.
Hands thrust into pockets.
Hand wringing.

(Contrast these hand gestures with rubbing together of hands or forming a "tent" with the fingers of both hands: these are *not* signals of objection, but firm "buy signals"; they invite you to push the sale toward a close.)

Respond to these verbal and nonverbal signals of *unexpressed* objection by making an effort to bring it to expression. You must uncover and defuse the hidden land mine. You cannot ignore it, hoping that you somehow won't stumble over it or that, if you do, it won't blow up.

If you have done your homework—know the merchandise and know your customers—you should have a list of anticipated objections already in your mind. Ask questions to get the prospect to put his objection(s) into words:

"How do you feel about the price?"
"Do you think we offer a good value?"
"Do you think our widget will solve your problem?"
"Do you think our widget will meet your needs?"
"Do you think our widget will meet your requirements?"
"What do you think about feature X?"
"Does the proposed schedule work for you?"
"What do you think of our guarantee and service plan?"
"Are you wondering how your customers/employees will respond to the
    X widget?"
"Do you have any questions or concerns about operating costs/
    maintenance costs/durability/the technology?"

If asking questions about the known or common issues that are likely to elicit objections fails to prompt your prospect to volunteer her objection(s), ask her for help:

"Have I left anything unanswered? Do you have any questions for me?"

"You seem hesitant. What questions have I left unanswered?"

"Help me to clear up any issues, any doubts."

"How can I help you make a decision today?"

"What information do I need to supply to help you make a decision?"

If you answer a stated objection, but the prospect is still hesitant to make the purchase, ask what other questions she has: "I'm glad I could clear that up. Now, tell me, what other questions can I answer about the X widget?" Keep asking questions until you get a buy signal, close the sale, or are given a definite no. Do not hesitate to elicit more objections. Remember, *expressed* objections are opportunities. *Unexpressed* objections—which are just as real—are land mines.

If the prospect fails to make his objections clear, do not lose patience, do not offer criticism, and never betray annoyance. Instead, help your prospect clarify: "So, if I'm hearing you correctly, you are not fully comfortable with the price. Is that correct?" Get the objection into the light, where you and your prospect can examine it together and resolve it.

Be aware that the two most common *unexpressed* objections are:

1. *Price too high.* Many people do not like (or are embarrassed) to admit that they cannot (or feel they cannot) afford something. If you anticipate or sense this as an objection, preempt the embarrassment in these ways:

   - "Some of my most loyal customers express hesitation about the price of the XYZ. I always suggest that they consider *value*, not just *cost*, and run the numbers for themselves. The XYZ, as you know, is the most energy-efficient widget available today. No competing unit offers comparable savings in operation."
   - "Managing costs is of course key to doing business today. That's why we offer in-house financing, which is quick, painless, and a very, very good deal."

2. *Prospect has other offers or is already working with someone else.* Some prospects like to tell you that you have competition for their business.

Others are hesitant or uncomfortable to reveal that they are looking at other products or other vendors or that they are already working with a vendor and are hesitant to switch to you. Give your prospect "permission" to reveal this information:

- "What other widgets have you considered?"
- "May I ask who your current supplier is?"

Again, you cannot compete if you don't know:

1. If you have competition.
2. What or who that competition is.
3. What the competing product or vendor offers.

More Questions

Here are some additional questions designed to transform unexpressed objections into expressed objections:

"Have I missed anything? Please let me know. I want to be sure that I understand exactly what you need."

"You seem enthusiastic about the benefits of the XYZ, but I'm not sure I fully understand your remaining concerns. What information have I failed to supply? How can I help you make this decision?"

"Usually, when somebody says they need to 'think it over,' what they're telling me is that I haven't answered all their questions or addressed all their concerns. *Is* there something I've left unanswered?"

"Is there someone else who needs to see this presentation so that you can feel comfortable about making the decision?"

"I'm detecting a change in your level of enthusiasm. Is it something I said—or didn't say? I'd hate to leave you with any misunderstanding or misinformation."

"Be honest now. You won't hurt my feelings. What do you think about the XYZ?"

"If you could change one thing about the ABC widget, what would it be?"

"Would you be interested in a no-obligation thirty-day free—and I do
　　mean *free*—trial?"

"What could I change in my presentation that would bring you to a
　　yes?"

"Is there anything else you'd like me to know?"

"What's stopping you from acting on this?"

PRICE-BASED OBJECTIONS

Objections based on price are so common that you should have a mental file of
answers ready. There are two reasons why the price-based objection is so frequently encountered. Number one, quality and value have a price, and it may
be relatively high. Number two, we are all culturally accustomed to bargain,
haggle, and negotiate. We tend to object to price even if the price seems right.
This said, *never* assume the price objection is a mere negotiating ploy. Always
acknowledge a price objection as a sincere concern and respond to it as such.

Never ignore the issue of price. It is, after all, important to your customer
and, for that matter, important to you. This said, never sell on the basis of
price. The price is a fact—not a feature and not even a benefit. Instead, sell
value, which is the ratio of price to benefit. Be as specific as you can in selling
value. If, in fact, your product or service is more expensive than the competition's, do not try to evade or gloss over this fact. Instead, explain it in terms
of value, including quality, range of features and benefits, innovative technology, longevity, potential for creating satisfaction, and so on. Reveal the *ap-
parently* unfavorable price comparison as a *positive*: evidence of higher
quality. Be sure to tout any awards, testimonials, test results, and other man-
ifestly objective evidence of the superiority and superior value of your product or service. Speaking of objective evidence, whenever possible, demonstrate
to the prospect the "true" cost of the merchandise—its value—by breaking
down cost over time: "Yes, our competitor comes in at $XX less than we do,
but over X years, the actual cost of using the competing product amounts to
$XX per month, while operating ours comes in at an average of just $X."

Do what you can to make price less of an issue. Offer a discount, if you have the authority to do so, or break down payments over time. Always emphasize *investment* over *cost* or *price*.

Give your prospect "permission" to feel okay—even *good*—about investing in your merchandise: "You know, Ms. Smith, we all experience a certain amount of stress when we invest money in a an important purchase like this. But you can feel very good about investing in the best value on the market today. What is more, you will feel good every time you use it."

EXAMPLE

John, you are absolutely right. This <type of service> requires a substantial investment. It is an important investment. That is a fact, and it is not subject to debate. But I do want to remind you that the costs of failing to perform this <type of service> in a high-quality manner are far, far higher. The liabilities are scary: <list them>. Now, we don't sell insurance. We sell something even better: *prevention*. And we do so through state-of-the-art technology and methods. You can put a price on your business. We protect that. It's much harder to put a price on your peace of mind. But we protect that, too. So, please, consider this as you make your decision.

ANOTHER EXAMPLE

I agree that $XXX is a substantial amount of money. But is it "too high" a *cost*? That really isn't the question we should be asking in order to make this decision. The relevant issue is not *cost*. That's just a number. The crucial issue is *value*, which tells you what your investment actually buys for you. Now, I'm not going to give you my opinion, because you know it's biased. But let me show you three statements from current clients:
<Testimonial 1>
<Testimonial 2>
<Testimonial 3>
Judge for yourself. These and other industry leaders know that serious value requires a serious investment. Fail to make the investment, and who knows what your "costs" will ultimately add up to.

WORDS AND PHRASES TO USE

Base your decision on projected results/revenue/savings

Cost is a concern but what value do you place on the benefits we discussed?

Durable

Easy terms

Free shipping/trial

Guarantee

How would you feel if you could own this for . . .

Investment

Look at the results we project

Results

Sound investment

The older unit required X percent more time than the new product

This is something that will give you satisfaction for years to come

Value more than justifies the price

What if I could deliver this to you at last year's price?

Will save X percent on operating costs

WORDS AND PHRASES TO AVOID

Cut-rate

Don't cheap out

Nothing I can do about price

Penny-wise, pound foolish

Quality costs

That is our pricing policy

This is no time to skimp

You can't get something for nothing

QUALITY-BASED OBJECTIONS

Another common objection is based on the quality or perceived quality of the product or service. Listen to the objection and attempt to meet and overcome it on its own terms. Your most effective counter is objective evidence, which includes reviews, customer testimonials, and, where appropriate, information about manufacturing, including ratings and certifications, especially by recognized impartial organizations, such as the International Standards Organization (ISO). Don't forget to highlight the quality of materials used. In the case of services, emphasize the training, experience, certifications, memberships, and awards of your service personnel.

One of the prime gotchas of quality-based objections is a price that seems *too low* and therefore suggests cut corners and compromised quality. Provide assurance of your company's commitment to provide value, which means never compromising quality. Explain the efficiencies employed to reduce costs without diminishing quality.

EXAMPLE

My friend, you are suffering from a disease that is very common among my customers. It's called the "Too Good to Be True" Syndrome, and it hits them when they see our low prices. The two symptoms of the syndrome are utter disbelief and an absolute conviction that a widget this inexpensive cannot be of high quality. Well, fortunately, the syndrome is 100 percent curable. Just compare our specs to those of our competitors. We use the same materials—better, in many cases—and we have a technology that is second to none. One thing we have focused on is manufacturing, in our ISO-certified plant, using advanced robotics that not only increase mechanical precision but greatly reduce the number of rejects and returns. Together, these techniques allow us to create the highest quality while keeping prices very low. That's how we do it.

ANOTHER EXAMPLE

I understand your doubt, and it's a good doubt to have. After all, if something seems too good to be true, it probably is. But just consider what it is you buy when you purchase from some of my high-priced competitors. They charge *you* for *their* fancy packaging, fancy offices, fancy retail space, and high-priced ads and commercials. Since *we* don't spend money on any of this, we don't have to charge *you* for it. Now, as for quality, I will tell you that the best of my competitors produces a good, reliable product. It is, however, priced substantially higher than my product, which is every bit as good. On quality, we never compromise. The product is the thing you keep and use. The packaging? You throw it all away. The offices? The ads? Do *you* really care about them?

WORDS AND PHRASES TO USE

Authentic

Authoritative

Breakthrough in quality

Brilliant

Buy the best

Cannot be improved

Certified

Commitment to quality

Craftsmanship

Cutting edge

Enduring

Genuine article

Get the best

Handmade

Highest grade available

Incomparable

Individually inspected

Investment-quality

Legacy

Long recognized as the best/the
   world's finest

Made in the USA

Masterpiece of the craft

Museum-quality

No finer

Obsessed with quality

Possess the best/finest

Precision

Proven excellence

Quality breakthrough

Real thing

State of the art

This is it

Touch of brilliance

Tradition of craftsmanship/value

Treasure

WORDS AND PHRASES TO AVOID

Acceptable

Be realistic

Bells and whistles

Can't do it

Don't expect a miracle

Make the compromise

No frills

Not at that price

You can't expect everything

You can't have it all

You can't have it your way all
   the time

NEED-BASED OBJECTIONS

One of the more challenging objections you will doubtless encounter is the prospect's protest that he simply does not *need* what you are selling. He may be right, but then again, he may only *think* or *believe* he does not need it. It is your job to try to persuade him otherwise. It is also important to recognize this objection for what it *may* actually be: the prospect's admission that he does not *need* the product, but also an indication that he really *wants* it. Nobody *needs* a Mercedes, Lexus, BMW, or Porsche, but a lot of us really do *want* one.

EXAMPLE

No argument. Investing in a premium widget is a luxury. It is an investment in pure pleasure and self-indulgence. Most people, it's true, would not call it a necessity. Honestly, I'm not so sure. Look, I do understand why you are hesitating. There are a dozen, maybe a hundred, more utilitarian or practical things you could buy. Maybe you even *need* some of these. But have you ever thought that you may also *need* to do yourself a favor? Always seemed to me that feeling good is a great—and *very* necessary—value.

ANOTHER EXAMPLE

You make a good point. As you say, *If it ain't broke, why fix it?* The only problem I have with that is *Are you sure it ain't broke?*

Think about it. You did not get to be where you are today by indulging a leave-well-enough-alone attitude. I think I'm right in assuming that "good enough" just doesn't cut it with you. Complacency is stagnation, and stagnation is failure.

Of course, you can "get along" without our product. But, from all indications, you've never been content with simply "getting along." Let me ask you to review the benefits of replacing your current <product> with our new and innovative model: <list benefits>. Are you certain you want to "get along" without these?

AND ANOTHER

I don't doubt that you haven't received many calls for the XYZ, and I fully understand that you want to allocate your funds to the merchandise that's in greatest demand. But consider that we might be dealing with a "chicken and egg" situation here. You don't get many inquiries about XYZ precisely because you don't *stock* XYZ, and you don't stock it because you don't get many calls about it.

It's a vicious circle, and I'd like to offer you an opportunity to break out of it by letting us create a new market for you with our special XYZ website promotion. This will give the product the visibility necessary to drive demand. The website is free to use with your regular online campaigning. We want *you* to succeed with this product.

WORDS AND PHRASES TO USE

Accelerated production	Greater value
Act now	Higher value
Analyze	If not now, when?
Are you satisfied?	In half the time
At a time like this	Indulge yourself
At stake	It's your future
Be the first	Long-term strategy
Before it's too late	More benefits
Benefit of new technology	New technology
Big picture	Once-a-year event
Calculate the value	Reward yourself
Can you afford not to?	Shaping the future
Don't put it off	Strategic move/view/decision
Examine	The stakes are high
Flexible	Think in terms of value
Gives you the competitive edge	Time-wise solution

WORDS AND PHRASES TO AVOID

Bargain	Oh, go ahead
Be impulsive	Take the plunge
But you *want* it	Won't hurt
Can't hurt	You don't know what you need
Cost	You don't need an excuse
Excuse	You only *think* you don't need it
Low cost	You won't regret it

DON'T WANT TO SWITCH VENDORS

Loyalty and friendship are real, and these forces often drive a prospect's commitment to a vendor, thereby making it difficult for a new contender, like you, to capture some or all of the prospect's business. Chances are, however, that loyalty and friendship have less to do with a prospect's objection to switching vendors than a basic aversion to change. Most of us tend to be governed by a kind of inertia. We don't get moving or, if we are moving, we don't change course unless some strong external force acts on us. Meet this objection by giving your prospect some excellent reasons to make the switch.

EXAMPLE

I appreciate your reluctance to leave a vendor you're comfortable with, and I would not invest my time or prevail on yours if I weren't so thoroughly confident that I can supply you with a superior product and superior service, and that I can give you faster turnaround on delivery. And did I mention better prices? Well: I *can* give you better prices than your current vendor gives you.

I'm not asking for a contract. I'm asking for *one* purchase order. Give us a try. Fire us if you aren't satisfied. But you *will* be satisfied. I can promise you that we are highly motivated, and we will not disappoint you.

ANOTHER EXAMPLE

When I called you yesterday, Mr. Jackson, I was not aware that you had had an unsatisfactory experience with our firm some years back. We've made a lot of changes since then: basically, we operate under the same name but with completely new ownership, new management, and the new attitude that goes with them. This makes me especially hungry for the opportunity to demonstrate to you just *how* new we are.

I do not want to write off your business. I not only want to clear our name and prove our worth, I want to deliver a benefit to you. The fact is, I believe you are putting *yourself* at a disadvantage by not giving us a try. We are motivated to make you a very satisfied customer.

WORDS AND PHRASES TO USE

Absolute, total satisfaction

All night long

At your side

Available around the clock

Challenge us

Committed to you

Customer service

Customized for you

Dare us

Easy to order

Full service

Give us a try

Hands-on personal attention

Impeccable service

Individualized service

Just tell us what you want

Leave it to us

Let us help you

No compromises

On your side

One-stop shop

Passionate

Place yourself in our hands

Problem solvers

Ready for you now

There for you

Unparalleled service

Unrivaled in service

We can, we will

We install anywhere

We're committed

WORDS AND PHRASES TO AVOID

Change is good

Drop him

Our competitors are no good

Roll the dice

Shake it up

Take a chance

Take the risk

We're just as good

What are you
afraid of?

BUSINESS IS "OFF"

An all-too-common objection to a pitch is the protest that "business is off" or "down" or "flat." The opportunity this objection creates for you is to offer your help by promoting a product or service that promises to stimulate the prospect's business and increase her revenue. You should exercise any authority you have to extend generous discount and payment terms to a distressed customer—without, of course, unduly sacrificing your own margins or compromising your best credit practices.

EXAMPLE

I realize it's little comfort, but of course you're not alone in suffering through a dismal retail season. That, however, is precisely why I urge you to take a fresh look at our exciting fall line. We are confident that it will spike traffic at all of your locations, and what is more, I'm prepared to extend a generous discount and the very same payment terms we give to our longest-established customers.

As well, we can ship <quantity> units immediately. This will deliver the newest, most exciting experience to your customers right away. Can we talk about the offer?

WORDS AND PHRASES TO USE

Accommodate

Act

Agree

Alternative

Answer your objections

Appreciate

Approval

Assure

Authorization/Authorize/
    Authorized

Available for immediate shipment

Benefits

Challenge the status quo

Choice/Choose

Comfort

Competitors

Confidence/Confident

Confirm

Consider

Convenient

Convinced

Create a new market

Decide/Decision

Demand

Demonstrate

Desire

Discuss

Do something good for yourself

Do yourself a favor

Ensure

Exactly what you want

Expedite

Experience

Extend special terms

Fresh

Generous/Generous terms

Give us a try

Go that extra mile

Good news

Great product

Greatest value for your dollar

Help

Hold the prices promised/Hold
    the quantities promised

I understand completely
Immediately
Industry leaders
Inventory
Lead time
Let us help you
Liabilities
Lock in your order
Look forward to hearing from
    you/working with you
Low
Meet or exceed the specifications
Minimum
Move
Need
No later than
Partners
Percentage
Pleased
Pleasure
Possible
Price that's right for you
Production times
Productive
Promise
Proven winner
Pure pleasure
Put us to the test
Ready to ship

Real
Relationship
Reliability
Requirement
Right combination
Satisfaction/Satisfied
Save
Schedule
Serve
Serve your needs better
Service
Solve
Supply
Sure
Target
Target date
Terms
Testimonial
Time
Trust
Truth
Try
Understanding
Value
Very special wholesale price
We can
We don't want you to get shut out
Winner

WORDS AND PHRASES TO AVOID

Absolutely not
Can't argue with policy
Cannot
Impossible

Maybe you'd better not order
Not authorized to change
    policy
Problem for you

Sorry, it's our policy	Wait for demand to pick up
That's a good reason not to buy right now	We can't
	We're all in the same boat

NOT AUTHORIZED TO MAKE THE DECISION

The advance work you do in preparation for a corporate sales call should identify the person with the authority to make a purchasing decision and write a check. If it has failed to do this, you may well encounter the objection that the person you are pitching does not have the "authority" to buy. Seize the opportunity to reach the right person, but also take steps to build on the contact you have just made.

EXAMPLE

Thanks for letting me know that Ms. Parker is the one who makes the final purchasing decisions. If all I was really interested in was making a sale, I would hang up on you and call her right now. However, I really enjoyed talking to you about our product, and I believe that we have established a valuable understanding of one another. Certainly, it is clear to me that you appreciate our value proposition. So, rather than go straight to Ms. Parker, I'd like to give you the opportunity—if you want it—to make the connection and alert her to our product. I can promise you that she will be very grateful for the tip. I'll call her at the end of the week.

WORDS AND PHRASES TO USE

A new standard	Everybody needs a little help sometimes
Beats the competition	
Bigger and better	
Boost	Fascinate
Distinguish yourself	Gain the edge
Draw customers	Gets the job done
Easy	Go for the gold

Higher performance/
   High-performance
Improve performance
Increase traffic
Lift
New
Performance plus
Priced to compete
Profit
Refresh
Regain the edge

Reinvigorate
Revenue
Shot in the arm
Step up
Three reasons to buy
We understand
We're here to help
Wins the gold
You'll see the difference
Your customers will thank you

WORDS AND PHRASES TO AVOID

Blowout
Cheap
Don't whine
Don't wimp out
Go for broke

If you build it, they will come
Sell-out
Take a chance
Times are tough for all of us
We need the work

CHAPTER 6

Close It

In the classic 1992 movie made from playwright David Mamet's Broadway hit *Glengarry Glen Ross*, Blake, the sales director from hell played by Alec Baldwin, lectures his faltering real estate sales force, beginning by writing the letters A, B, C on a blackboard.

"Always Be Closing," he snarls.

It is one of the time-honored clichés of sales how-to manuals. The idea is that nothing you say to a prospect should be "wasted." Every word out of your mouth, every gesture you make, every breath you take should be single-mindedly directed at *closing* the sale.

There is certainly value in this approach, nasty as Baldwin's Blake is about it. Take care to promote the positive and to lead and to facilitate the prospect's journey toward a successful close. Avoid accidentally wandering into the territory of doubt and second thoughts. Create a good time, a pleasant experience, for you and your prospect, but don't fritter away time—yours and, even more important, the prospect's.

Nevertheless, the *ABC* formula risks tempting you to overlook another key formula. Call it *ABL&L*: Always Be Listening and Looking. If you interpret "Always Be Closing" to mean Always Be Talking, you cannot be doing much listening or looking. The common phrase "sales presentation" is something of a misnomer because, like *ABC*, it implies delivering a monologue, whereas successful selling is always interactive. Listening and responding are just as important as presenting. After you present your merchandise, after you have secured the prospect's attention, generated his interest, and stirred his desire for the product or service, it is time to listen and look attentively. What you seek are the prospect's signals that he is prepared to buy.

READ THE BUY SIGNALS

Sometimes, a prospect will simply tell you, "I'll take that" or "I'm ready to talk price" or "Let's make a deal." Often, however, the prospect will not be so straightforward. Even in these cases, however, she will typically send you "buy signals," verbal or visual cues—often a combination of the two—that she is ready to move to the close of the sale.

What to Listen For

Even if your prospect doesn't come out with "Let's make a deal," most buy signals are reasonably obvious. Very often, they come in the form of questions. Listen for any of these:

How much is that one?
What's the difference in price between model A and model B?
Do you have one in red?
What do you charge for delivery?
How soon can you ship?
What kind of financing do you offer?
How long does the job take?
Is there a warranty?
Okay. Is this your very best price?
What payment do you require up front?

When you receive signals like these, stop selling and start answering. Providing satisfactory information is usually sufficient to move the sale to a successful close.

Prospects to whom you are selling face-to-face may ask a companion for an opinion or approval. Or they may "phone a friend," taking out their cell phone to discuss the purchase with a friend or family member—and in some cases to get approval from someone, usually a boss, who must formally authorize the purchase. It is not uncommon for smartphone-equipped prospects to take a photograph or video of the merchandise in question and transmit it to a friend, family member, or employer for approval. It is possible, certainly, that the person on the other end of the line may turn thumbs down and discourage or even kill a sale. More often, however, the act of "phoning a friend" is a very positive buy signal. The prospect is not looking to be dissuaded from making the purchase but, on the contrary, wants affirmation of his decision to buy.

Don't obviously or blatantly eavesdrop on any conversation the prospect attempts to make private, but anything she says within your normal hearing is fair game. Listen for:

What do you think about it?
Should I do it?
Should I just go ahead?
Can we get this into the car?
Will this really match our sofa?
Does the price seem fair to you?

Just as savvy shoppers learn—or at least try to learn—to restrain any obvious displays of enthusiasm, you should resist the temptation to answer buy signal questions in ways that suggest any desperation to sell. Enthusiasm about the merchandise is great, but avoid appearing overly eager to unload your wares. For example, when asked "Is that your best price?" you may be tempted to push the sale by instantly offering a lower number. Don't do it. Instead, smile and answer, "Yes, it is—the very best price." This tells your customer, first, that you care enough about him to give him your best price; second, that you aren't holding out on him; and, third, that you are a person of honesty and integrity. To have responded by lowering your price would have suggested that you were being coy or outright deceptive at the start of the sale. Answering that you have given the customer the best price is actually a confidence builder and will assist toward closing the sale.

Here are more verbal cues to listen for:

1. Prospects who ask for "details" about a product—specifications, features, and so on—are moving toward a purchase decision. The more deeply they get into the details, the more interested they probably are.

2. Prospects who ask directly about price are confronting the reality of buying. If a particular item is in question, tell the prospect the price. If the question concerns a class of merchandise, consider asking the prospect what she was planning to spend. "If I have an idea of your range, I can help you find the best value for the money."

3. Prospects who tell you how they plan to use the product: "I'd use this instead of the old machine I have now." This is known as "possession language," and it means that the prospective customer is already thinking about ownership. Move in and encourage this kind of talk. Get the prospect accustomed to talking about the product as if he already owns it: "Oh, you're going to really enjoy using this. I just know it."

What to Look For

When you are in a retail selling situation, whether in a shop, an automobile dealership, or a convention showroom, pay close attention to the people wandering through. Not every one of them is a prospective customer, but every one of them does send signals. They range from "I have no real interest in buying anything" to "I want to buy, and I want to buy *now*," as well as attitudes in between these extremes, including "I'm interested in the product, but I'm currently not ready to buy" and "I might buy, if I can get my questions answered and my doubts addressed."

Let's begin with the common not-ready-to-buy signals. They are important to recognize because, if you are on a busy sales floor or in a crowded show, you may not want to invest much time with prospects who are not likely to become customers. Instead, you will want to focus on the prospects who signal that they are most likely to buy. If you do have the time to devote to reluctant or undecided customers, it is best to be able to assess their opening level of interest (or lack thereof), so that you can formulate an effective approach. Finally, if you are already engaged in a sales presentation with a customer, you need to recognize the signs of waning interest or growing doubt so that you can ask questions aimed at increasing interest and alleviating doubt.

The most common nonverbal no-buy signal is deliberate avoidance of eye contact. Look directly at the prospect. If she looks away, she probably does not want to be approached. If you are already engaged in a sales presentation and the prospect begins avoiding eye contact, take steps to reengage interest. Ask:

> "I'm getting the feeling that you have questions I've not answered. Am I
> right?"
> Or: "Is there something I'm leaving out?"
> Or: "You seem bothered by something. What is it?"
> Or: "What are your remaining concerns?"

Also consult Chapter 5 on overcoming objections and on asking questions to bring hidden objections out into the open.

Another common nonverbal no-buy signal is the idle or casual picking up and handling of different products. If the prospect seems genuinely interested in the merchandise, offer to help. If, however, the behavior appears to be fidgeting, his handling of the merchandise automatic and thoughtless, the prospect is probably just killing time and is not actually interested in making a purchase. The same is true for a prospect who walks through a sales area and hurriedly looks at many different products. Generally speaking, well-motivated buyers tend to zero in on a product or category of product that genuinely interests them.

You can often gauge the waxing and waning interest of a prospect in the course of a sales presentation by watching body language. Danger signals—no-buy signals, signals that you are losing the prospect—include:

1. Fidgeting—indicates boredom and/or dissatisfaction with what you are saying.
2. Sighing—a sign of frustration and even exasperation.
3. Head scratching—puzzlement, noncomprehension.
4. Lip biting—the prospect has been made anxious by something you've said.
5. Rubbing the back of the neck—generally conveys frustration and impatience.
6. Narrowing of the eyes—a strong negative gesture suggesting hard disagreement, possibly even resentment or anger.
7. Raising the eyebrows—generally conveys disbelief.
8. Peering over the top of the eyeglasses—another signal that what you are saying is not being accepted as honest.
9. Crossing arms in front of the chest—defiance, extreme resistance.
10. Rubbing eyes, ears, or side of nose—doubt, perhaps about the merchandise or you, or self-doubt on the part of the prospect.

When you pick up on these—or any gestures that suggest that the prospect is uncomfortable and unhappy—offer help. Ask the prospect if he has any unanswered questions. If he seems particularly doubtful or even upset, say, "Something I've said—or have not explained—seems to be bothering you. What is it? Let me help."

Now on to buy signals or, at least, signals of interest. Always look for the following:

1. The prospect spends time looking at one product, product type, or one page or section of a catalog or sales brochure. Don't interrupt, but do offer help: "I see you are looking at our widgets. Is there anything I can help you with in terms of providing information or advice?"
2. Be aware that the more time a prospect invests in one particular item or class of items, the more ready she is to buy.

3. On a sales floor, the prospect looks around, as if trying to find someone to help him. The obvious response is to offer help. If you are un-
   sure, however, just catch the person's gaze, raise your eyebrows a bit
   to signal that you are ready to help, and watch the response. If the
   prospect sustains her glance or raises her eyebrows, move in to close.

4. Watch for changes in body state. That is, if the prospect suddenly
   seems relaxed after asking you questions about the product, you can
   assume that he finds your answers satisfactory, his anxiety and doubts
   have been reduced, and he is moving toward actually making the purchase.

5. A prospect who reaches for his wallet or starts rummaging through
   her purse is probably getting ready to count cash or retrieve a credit
   card. "May I help you with this?" is an appropriate closing question in
   this case. If the credit card is already out, offer your hand to take it.
   Keep further sales talk to a minimum. You don't want to "unsell" the
   product.

WORDS AND PHRASES TO USE

Absolute

Accessories

Accommodate

Act

Agree

Alternative

Answer

Answer your objections

Appreciate

Appropriate

Approval

Assure

Authorization/Authorize/
   Authorized

Available for immediate shipment

Benefits

Challenge the status quo

Choice

Choose

Comfort

Confirm our understanding

Create a new market

Deadline

Debate

Decide/Decision

Demand has been unusually high

Demonstrate

Desire

Direct/Directly

Discuss

Do something good for
   yourself

Enjoy/Enjoyable/Exactly what
  you want
Expedite
Experience
Extend special terms
Features
Final
Follow-up
Fresh
Furnish
Give us a try
Good news
Great product
Greatest value for your dollar
Guarantee
Industry leader
Information
Lock in your order
Look forward to hearing from
  you/working with you
No compromise on quality
Price that's right for you
Production times
Proven winner

Pure pleasure
Right combination
Satisfaction/Satisfied
Save
Schedule
Serve/Service
Serve your needs better
Solve
Sophisticated
Style
Substantial
Supply
Sure
Testimonial
Trust/Truth
Try
Understanding
Value
Vendor
Very special price
We can
We don't want you to get shut out
Winner
Yes

WORDS AND PHRASES TO AVOID

Come on
Don't be foolish and miss an
  opportunity
Don't fail to make the right choice
I need to wrap this up
Just do it
Just trust me
Take my word for it

The time for a decision is
  right now
There's no room for negotiation
This is the only chance
  you'll get
This is the opportunity of a
  lifetime
We're running out of time

Would I lie to you?   You need to make a decision
You have to buy this   You would be crazy not to

PROVOKE A BUY SIGNAL

If a prospect conveys neither buy nor no-buy signals, attempt to elicit or provoke a buy signal by asking some of the questions suggested in Chapter 5 to overcome objections. Often, a simple "May I help you?" or, even better, "How may I help you?" is all that is needed. ("May I help you?" invites a quick yes or no, whereas "How may I help you?" calls for a brief conversation.) If you are making a presentation and get no discernible response, ask:

"What questions do you have for me?"
Or: "What haven't I covered?"
Or: "Is there something that interests or concerns you that I haven't
     addressed?"

Another approach is to ask a rhetorical question. Suppose that the prospect has been looking at a product for a time, but has given no significant buy signals beyond this. Approach and ask, "Isn't that beautiful?" Or say: "That is one our bestsellers." Or: "People really respond to this one."

You should also learn to recognize when a prospect is at what might be called the "hesitation point." Frequently, this point is reached when you are presenting a range of products or options to a prospect. You begin with the highest-priced product or option. The prospect rejects the item because of price. You step down in price and again meet with rejection. At some point, as you descend in price, you may find that the prospect stops rejecting the merchandise, but still hesitates. At this "hesitation point," do what you can to close the sale. This includes asking questions to overcome resistance (as in Chapter 5), offering better payment terms, removing one option to lower the price a bit more, and so on. Only if the sale is finally rejected should you move to an even lower-priced item or option.

Depending on what you are selling, you may not need or want to actually show each level of product. You may instead begin by simply *discussing* the available range, starting with the highest. If the prospect rejects this, talk about the next lower. Watch and listen for buy signals before descending again.

People often insist that they have a maximum budget for an item; however, in many cases, they will go above this if they feel—that is, if you persuade them—that the product is worth it. If you start by showing or discussing the high end of a range first, you create an index or standard against which the prospect can compare lesser offerings. In many instances, those lower-priced items make the high-end model look more desirable and more like a very good value. Indeed, moving your prospect from thinking in terms of price to thinking instead in terms of value is often a big step toward closing the sale.

Here is an example of moving a prospect off the hesitation point and provoking a buy signal:

> The XYZ models start at $500. [*Pause long enough to gauge reaction. Prospect folds his arms across his chest, a no-buy signal.*] That represents a substantial investment, of course, and if you would like something of nearly equivalent value for your money, I'd recommend considering the WXY range of models, which begin at $375. Does that make sense to you? [*Prospect replies that it is still too pricey.*] The best value we can deliver is a refurbished WXY14, fully factory guaranteed, which is priced at $285. [*There is hesitation, but no explicit protest or obviously resistant body language.*] Let me show you the item. *This* is the best value for the features you want.

WORDS AND PHRASES TO USE

A greater value than you may
    think
A true pleasure to use
Absolute guarantee
Access
Acknowledged leader
All necessary certifications
American-made

Anytime/anyplace/anywhere
Approved
Assembles in minutes
At the touch of your
    fingertips
Call us
Complete instructions
Convenient

Conveniently located
Critics' choice
Easier than you think
Easy to care for
Effortless action
Fully compliant
I bet you can't wait to start
  using it
I can show you
Just one glance
Laboratory tested
No problem
Original
Practical

Proudly made right here in
  the USA
Quick and easy
Ready to use
Real-world/Real world–tested
Right out of the box
Seal of approval
Service guarantee
Simple
Snap
The market leader
The pacesetter others follow
Top-rated
We'll do all the paperwork for you

WORDS AND PHRASES TO AVOID

Adequate
All these things are pretty much
  the same
As good as the rest
Bare minimum
Bare-bones
Bargain price
Cheap labor
No difference
Not very exciting
Outsourced

People seem to like it
Quick and dirty
Rock bottom
Standard
We think it's good
What do you expect for the
  money?
You can't afford better
You've seen one, you've seen
  them all

CLOSE IT

When the prospect is clearly ready to act, to make the purchase—expedite the process. Don't rush. Don't push. Don't engage in commentary or small talk. The best way to proceed is to express pleasure—not gratitude, not relief, but pleasure:

"Splendid!"
"Great!"
"Excellent!"
"Terrific!"
"Spectacular!"

Then deliver a *short* affirmation of the customer's decision:

"Excellent choice."
"Fine choice."
"Ah, a wise decision."
"You will enjoy this."
"This will do the job for you."

At this point in the sales process, the prospect becomes a customer, and your responsibility now is not to make the sale—the sale is made—but to begin delivering excellent customer service. This means completing the sale as expeditiously as possible. If there are forms to fill out or essential information required from the customer, you should do as much of the work as possible. In general, avoid making your customer work to obtain his merchandise. If your company wants you to collect additional, nonessential survey-type information from the customer, do *not* apologize for this part of the process or imply that it is an imposition on the customer's time—though it may well be. Instead, *ask* permission to take a few moments (if possible, give a realistic estimate of the amount of time required) to ask a few questions "that will help us to serve you most efficiently in the future" or "that will help us to support your product more effectively." If the customer protests that she doesn't have time, reply, "I understand," and let the matter drop. This said, most customers will respond positively to a reasonable request for their time, provided that it is believably framed not as something *you* want from them, but as a value-added service you perform *for them*.

WORDS AND PHRASES TO USE

Added value	Appreciate
An exceptional value	Best prices always

Congratulations!
Cool!
Excellent!
Exclusive
Express checkout
For your benefit
Great choice!
Great unit
Hassle-free
Just one more question
Just one more signature
Let me help you
Low cost of operation
Most-favored customer

Nice price
No hassle
Perfect for you
Permission
Right decision
Super choice!
Terrific service
The most popular choice
Useful to you
We're almost done
Well done!
Wonderful!
You will be glad you did
You will enjoy it

WORDS AND PHRASES TO AVOID

Customer's always right
Decent value
Hurry along, please
I don't use it myself
I have not *heard* any complaints
I hope you don't mind
I know some people who use it
I must ask you these questions
Limited
Long form

Sorry
Sorry for the inconvenience
Sorry to bother you
They make me ask
This is company policy
We all march to a different
  drummer
We have had a few complaints
You get what you pay for
You must fill out this form

PART TWO

MASTER THE SITUATION

The chapters in this part break down selling into the six most common scenarios: selling to your current customers; selling in the retail environment; selling to a purchasing manager in a business-to-business context; and selling to the corporate executive, the entrepreneur or small business owner, and the professional.

CHAPTER 7

Sell Your Best Prospect

Sales personnel will move heaven and earth to find new customers. Such zeal is laudable—unless it causes you to overlook your very best prospects of all: your current customers. Failing to make additional sales from them because you are too busy looking for new customers is like neglecting to look after and invest the money you have because you are too busy trying to make more. Your current customers represent a valuable asset. Grow that asset.

WHY YOUR CURRENT CUSTOMERS ARE YOUR BEST PROSPECTS

Marketing experts and corporate brand managers talk a lot about "brand equity." The proven appeal of a well-known brand, brand equity typically takes years to develop. Coca-Cola is a famous example of brand equity. A lot of people worldwide love Coke, and they are therefore likely not only to remain loyal to that particular soft drink, but to give *any* beverage (and even some other products as well) that bears the Coca-Cola brand a try. The people at

Coca-Cola devote a great deal of effort to protecting and to nurturing their enormous brand equity. They understand that it's the lifeblood of the company.

Think of your current customers as people who recognize and have already invested in the equity of your firm's brand. Your enterprise has proved itself to them, at least to some degree. These customers have invested their time, cash, and—again, at least to some degree—their reputation in you, your merchandise, and your firm. You owe them something. You owe them the opportunity to derive even more value, more benefits, from you and your firm in the form of additional products and services. Pay your current customers back by serving them, cultivating them, and growing business from them. Pay them back by selling more to them.

SPEAK THE LANGUAGE OF NURTURE

These days, a great many successful companies watch us all very closely. Anything we buy online is tracked and recorded. Much of what we purchase from brick-and-mortar stores is also reduced to data, processed, and used. This is why so many of us get a regular daily ration of emails that start off with something like "As a customer who has recently purchased XYZ, you may also be interested in ABC." Some of us find such messages annoying and intrusive; most of us just ignore and delete them—but a few of us actually appreciate them for alerting us to new products we may actually benefit from.

The impulse behind blasting sales-related emails to established customers is a very good one. Unfortunately, the great majority of these messages are impersonal and even exploitive. That is, they come across as nothing more than ways to address the need of the *seller* (which is, of course, to sell) rather than the needs and wants of the *buyer*—which are ultimately about obtaining high value by acquiring the benefits of a product or a service. The sales professionals who take the time and effort to communicate with their established customers in the *language of nurture*, a language that focuses on the customer's needs and wants, have a significant edge over the individuals and companies that use only the *language of gimme*, which is about selling and nothing more than selling. Use the language of nurture, and your established customers will appreciate being informed about new products and services of interest to them. Churn out the language of gimme, however, and they will ignore your messages or, even worse, be annoyed and alienated by them.

EXAMPLES

Phone Call

YOU: Hi, Frank, it's Ted Williams at Magic Audio. Are those RXY speakers you bought from me last year everything you hoped they'd be?

CUSTOMER: I love 'em.

YOU: Well, I knew you would, and I'm just calling to tell you that we are now handling the BoomIt line of subwoofers. I'm thinking that BoomIt's Model Y would complement the sound of your RXYs perfectly—really fill out the low, low end of the music without stepping on the ranges in which your RXYs excel so brilliantly.

CUSTOMER: Do I really need something like that?

YOU: Depends on how much impact and fidelity you want. You've made a commitment to great hi-fi with those RXYs. A BoomIt is the next logical step up.

CUSTOMER: So what's the cost?

YOU: The Model Y is $XXX.

CUSTOMER: Ouch . . .

YOU: Compare other high-end subwoofers, which go well into the thousands, Frank.

CUSTOMER: Oh, I know, but that's still more than I can put into my equipment right now.

YOU: Frank, BoomIt has other, lower-cost options that could work for you as well. But, of course, only you can tell. Can I suggest that you drop by? I'll hook up several BoomIt models with a pair of RXYs, just like yours. Take a listen. Judge for yourself.

CUSTOMER: Look, are you going to be in the store this weekend?

YOU: Sure will. See you then?

Email

Clara,

It's been quite a while since we worked together on product promotions for your shop, so I thought you would like to see some of our recent online work.

The first link below will take you to a campaign we did for a mortgage company. Bumped their click-through rate up by 97 percent. The second link will bring up work we did for General Insurance Providers to generate consumer inquiries about their new identity theft insurance offerings. They've come back to us three times now for more, so we must be doing something right.

I'd love to sit down with you to hear what you guys are getting into next and to talk about what we might be able to do to help with targeted web ads that will click through directly to your selling site. You already know we're all about value and service, so just give me an appointment, and I can be at your door anytime.

All best,
Ben

WORDS AND PHRASES TO USE

A jump on the competition
A real time-saver
Able to inspire others
Advanced/Advancement
Anticipate
At a time like this
Build on what you have
Contemporary vision
Cutting edge
Desirable upgrade
Don't put it off
Enhance your prestige/your system
Even better

Evolutionary
Exciting
Expand
Forward-thinking
Fully tested
Future
Give you the edge
Gives you an early start
Highest technology
Imagine
Improved/Improvement
Inspiring
It's your future
Just imagine

Major advantage
Meet your needs now and for the
    future
Most important/significant in
    years
Must-have upgrade
Next move/Next step/Next thing
Proactive
Professional tool
Protect your investment
Put it to the test
Revolutionary
Shaping the future
Significant upgrade
Technology

The buzz
The future
The moment has arrived
The one everybody's talking about
Think ahead
This is it/the one/the ultimate
Time for a change
Time-tested but new
Upgrade
We're excited about this new
    product/new service
When your future's on the line
Why put it off?
Will withstand the test of time

WORDS AND PHRASES TO AVOID

A steal
Are you still using that old
    thing?
Bargain of the century
Because it's new
Better rush
Better than what you've got
Don't be a loser/Don't lose out
Fad

Giving it away
Need a decision today
Well, it's new
Won't last long
You can't lose
You have to have whatever
    is new
Your competition is breathing
    down your neck

SPEAK THE LANGUAGE OF REPAIR

Obviously, it is easier to appeal successfully to an *existing* customer who is also a *satisfied* customer. In the real world, however, even the best companies, companies that consistently deliver high value and first-rate quality, fail to satisfy all of their customers all of the time. In Chapter 17, we will present detailed strategies for converting customer complaints into opportunities to create satisfaction; however, it is useful here to understand that, just as there is a *language of nurture* to build and increase the loyalty of customers whom you have satisfied in the past, there is also a *language of repair* to create satisfaction among dissatisfied existing customers.

Here's the scenario: You call or email an existing customer, hoping to make a new sale. Instead, you get hit with a complaint in return. You have four choices of response:

1. Get defensive.
2. Just ignore the complaint.
3. Groan loudly and grudgingly address the complaint.
4. Offer help.

If you want to keep—or, in fact, to reactivate—this customer, you'll choose option 4. If you want to stay in business, you'll choose option 4 *each and every time* a situation like this presents itself.

Do your best to start thinking of customer complaints not as evidence that your product or service has failed, but as opportunities to promote yourself and your company by offering three things of great value:

1. A sincere apology
2. Empathy with the customer
3. Your assistance

Speaking the language of repair is meant to give your customer the feeling that you and your company really do care about her. Nowhere is this more critical than in communication that addresses a complaint or problem. You want your customer to come away from the encounter with you thinking, *Well, I did have a problem with the widget, but Mary at ABC Widgets moved heaven and earth to make it right.* What is more, you want your customer to think this *and* to tell this to others: "You know, they did make a mistake, but they fixed it, and they really made sure I was satisfied. You don't see that kind of integrity and personal attention much these days."

Get your customer to think along these lines, and you've done more than fix a problem. You've sold your customer on your company.

EXAMPLES

Phone Call

CUSTOMER: Well, it's very nice that you'd like to sell me the new model, but I have to tell you the one I've got has never worked the way I expected it to. It's acceptable, I guess, but I'm not really satisfied, and I don't know that I want to risk investing in the upgrade.

YOU: I am very sorry to hear this, Ms. Wilson. I was not aware that you were dissatisfied, and I wish you would have let us know right away, so that we could have given you immediate assistance. Can you tell me what the problems are?

CUSTOMER: [*Details a few complaints.*]

YOU: Again, I apologize. I can offer you two options to make things not just better, but to make things right. I can email to you an expedited RMA number plus a paid shipping label to our service department. We will examine the device at no charge, and we will repair or replace anything covered by the warranty, which is still in force. Alternatively, I can express-ship our new model on a thirty-day trial. You pay nothing up front. If you are pleased with the new model and its many improvements—as I really believe you will be—I will be happy to extend to you the current promotional price of $XXX. If you decide not to purchase the new model, just call me, I'll send you a paid return label, and you can also send in your current unit for warranty inspection and, if appropriate, repair. How does that sound to you?

CUSTOMER: I have to admit, it sounds more than fair.

YOU: We want you to be satisfied, totally satisfied. Nothing less will satisfy *us*. Now, would you like to try the new model for thirty days?

Email

Dear Mr. Smith,

Thank you for responding to my email offering you an upgrade to the XYZ Widget.

I am very sorry that you had a problem with your shipment back when you ordered your current unit, and that the partial shipment we made at that time caused you inconvenience. Let me assure you that, while such poor performance is obviously unacceptable, it is also very rare. Challenge us with a new order—for the upgrade—and I promise that you will not be disappointed. In fact, I will offer you expedited overnight shipping at no cost to you at all.

Let me thank you for your patience and understanding, and just fill out the information requested below. We will ship the upgrade to you overnight.

Whatever you decide, please let me express my gratitude to you for being a great customer.

Cordially,

Another Email

Dear Jane Kirk,

I can well appreciate your frustration over the repeated unavailability of the Wonder Widget last April. We did have problems with one of our key suppliers, and I fully understand your aggravation. Let me assure you that, with the Wonder 2.0, we have had absolutely no supplier problems, despite incredible customer demand.

I'll be straight with you. I would really love to sell you the 2.0, because I know you will be delighted with it. But I am much more concerned that your previous experience with us was less than 100 percent satisfying. If you give us another chance to prove that we deliver what we promise, I'll deliver it to you for free. The shipping's on us, and it will go out within 24 hours of receiving your order.

Please email me or call on my direct line—555-555-5555—if you have any questions at all. And thanks for taking the time to tell me about the problem last April.

All best,

WORDS AND PHRASES TO USE

100 percent satisfied

Absolutely

Accuracy

Advantage

Advise me on how you would like
   to proceed

Agree

Alternative

Appreciate the points you raise/
   your good humor

As soon as possible

At no charge

Attractive price

Bargain

Best option

Choice is yours

Competitive

Complete satisfaction

Confidence

Confirmation

Coordinate our resources

Decision you will be happy with

Delighted

Desirable

Develop

Direct line

Double-check

Durability

Effective

Efficiently

Effort

Eligible

Enhance/Enhancement

Ensure that it is given prompt
   attention

Estimate

Exactly what you need

Examine

Exchange

Expectations

Expedite delivery

Experience

Express my gratitude/my thanks

Far exceeded our expectations

Flexibility

Formulate strategy

Free

Frustration

Full exchange value

Fully

Future

Golden opportunity

Great product features

Greatly value your business

Happy to exchange/to help

Helpful

Honor

Hope

I agree

I am prepared

Immediate

Imperative

Important

Improved

In accordance with the terms
   agreed upon

In most cases

Information

Informative

Make every effort

Make things right

Minimize inconvenience

Minimum of delay

Miscommunication

Mistake

Misunderstanding

Mobilize all our forces

My attention

Necessary

New

Nominal charge

Offer

Offer my apologies

Opportunity

Optimal

Options

Our job is to help you

Perfect accuracy

Perform

Personal apology/attention

Possible

Powerful

Privilege

Promise

Prompt/Promptly

Prompt cash refund

Propose

Questions

Quickly and accurately

Receive

Recommend/Recommended

Rectify the error

Regret

Reimburse

Reserve

Resolve

Responsive

Review

Sales agreement

Satisfaction

Save

Scrupulously honest

Service at no charge

Share

Should resolve the problem

Significant

Sincere apology

Sorry

Sorry to hear

Sorry you find that unacceptable

Suggest/Suggestion

Suitable

Test

Thank you for calling me

Thoroughly test/tested

Timely and efficient

Trade-in value

Trouble-free

Trust you will find this
    satisfactory

Unavailable

Unavoidable

Understand your confusion

Up and running

Upgrade/Upgraded

What would you suggest?

Why not call?

Wonderful

You have made a great
    choice

WORDS AND PHRASES TO AVOID

Can't help

Can't hit a home run every time

Can't please everyone

Company policy

I find that hard to believe

It was inspected

Look at it from my point
    of view

Make do

No one else has ever had this
    problem

Nobody's perfect

Not our fault

Not our problem

Oh, sorry. I won't bother you
    again.

Sorry, but there's nothing we
    can do

Strict company policy

That was another salesperson

That's a pity

That's another department

That's our policy

That's the way it is

These things happen

Too bad

Try to understand

Unrealistic expectations

User error

We can't be responsible

We do our best

We try

What do you expect?

You expect too much

You must be doing something
    wrong

UPGRADE AND UPSELL

Established customers are often obvious candidates for upgrades and upselling—the purchase of more advanced, more fully featured, and more expensive products and services than they now own or use. The art of upgrading and upselling, however, is to do so without making your prospective repeat customer feel dissatisfied with the purchase he currently has. You want to build on his present satisfaction, not imply that what he has bought from you previously is actually somehow inferior.

To preserve a relationship of integrity and credibility, steer clear of "hard sell" tactics—the suggestion, for instance, that you are presenting a once-in-a-lifetime offer. The best tone to adopt, whether in a phone call or an email, is informational. You are giving your customer something very valuable: new information about a product or service that will benefit her.

Structurally, the most effective way to approach this communication is to begin by establishing the customer's need for accessories, upgrades, or related products. One effective approach is to explain to the customer how the upgrade or accessory will enhance or otherwise protect her initial investment in the original product, perhaps by expanding its capabilities or improving its operation.

After you have established a need for the item or service, develop the customer's interest in your offering. Be certain to anticipate possible objections. It is always advisable to emphasize the value—the cost-effectiveness—of the new product or service.

Finally, you must prompt the customer to act. Close the sale by explaining to her how to place an order or how to obtain additional information.

EXAMPLES

Phone Call

YOU: Hello, <customer name>. This is <your name> at <your company>. I have some exciting news about a product <or product line> you, as a current user of <product>, will want to know about. Would you like to hear it?

CUSTOMER: Yes.

YOU: <Product 1> is a great add-on to your <product> because it will allow you to <describe benefit> and to make more cost-effective use of your <product>. It is a great way to make the most of your wise initial investment. <Product 2> is for users who <describe need or use>. With this add-on, you can customize the output from your <product> in the following ways: <list them>. Do either—or both—of these new products seem like add-ons that will be of value to you?

CUSTOMER: Well, what kind of prices are we talking about?

YOU: <Product 1> is priced at $XX. We estimate that it will save you $XX per year in energy costs. Also, because it gives your <product> greater flexibility, you are will be significantly increasing the value of your purchase. <Product 2> is priced at $XX, and gives you the value of customization and personalization in so many ways. I think you'll agree that these both represent excellent values.

Email 1

Dear <name>:

We at <name of company> are always eager to give your <product> professional maintenance, but we also encourage user self-maintenance as an even more cost-effective alternative for our valued customers. For this reason, we stock a full line of spare parts, each of which comes with complete installation instructions.

For your unit, we recommend that you keep the following spare parts on hand: <list>. Having them on hand will hold any possible downtime to a minimum.

If you would like to place an order, just click on this link: <link to website>.

Email 2

Dear <name>:

We're absolutely certain that you are enjoying and benefitting from your new <product 1>—which is why we want to tell you about <product 2>. It substantially increases the functionality and convenience of <product 1> at a modest cost by delivering the following benefits: <list>

If you want to enjoy the added advantages of <product 2>, just click on <link>, which will take you to our Valued Customer Expedited Order site. Any questions? Email me at <address> or call 555-555-5555.

Email 3

Dear <name>:

When you purchased your <product>, we made a pledge to protect your investment. One important way in which we keep our promise to you is to make certain that you are always on the leading edge of technology, and that means giving you the opportunity to purchase at very special prices product upgrades and improvements as we develop them.

Our new <upgrade product> is one of the most exciting upgrades we have ever developed. It includes a wealth of new features, such as: <list>

Best of all, it is available to owners of <product> for only $XX—a savings of $X off the regular retail price.

I urge you urge to take advantage of this special offer by clicking on <link>, which will take you to our secure Expedited Order website, which is reserved exclusively for our valued customers.

WORDS AND PHRASES TO USE

A leap ahead

A magnificent upgrade

A new twist

A popular upgrade

A revolutionary upgrade

A step ahead

A striking new addition

A true innovation

Adapted to your needs

Added value

Ahead of the pack

Be a pacesetter

Best-selling accessory

Breakthrough accessory

Entirely redesigned

Even better/more effective/more
　　versatile

Evolutionary

Expand

Extend

Extend the useful life of

Faster

First time ever

Fresh and creative

Highest value

Improve

Innovative

Make the most of

Never obsolete

Now the most advanced available

Our best discovery yet

Our most popular

Outstanding addition

Refresh

Renew	Unlike any other
Stay ahead	Updated
Take advantage of	Upgrade
Takes it one step further	Versatility
Ten times faster/stronger	Way ahead of the competition
The next level	You spoke, we listened

WORDS AND PHRASES TO AVOID

Better than it was	What we should have done in the first place
Fixed	
Pretty good	You will never need another
Take my word for it, you need this	You'll just hate what you have now
Throw the old one away	

PUT YOUR CURRENT CUSTOMER TO WORK

Even in this age of social media, word of mouth remains the most powerful weapon in the marketing and sales arsenal. The problem is that many of us find it difficult to ask for referrals, recommendations, and testimonials. This is because we tend to think of such requests as asking somebody to give us something for nothing. Make it easier on yourself by shifting your thinking. Look upon these requests as your offering someone an opportunity to help you. The fact is that most people enjoy helping others and are certainly flattered by being asked to lend their name, judgment, and approval to a product or service. If your product or service delivers a good value, you are giving your customer an opportunity not only to feel good about herself by helping you, but also to feel good about helping her friends by introducing them to you, your company, and what you have to offer. To ask someone for a recommendation or testimonial is actually to honor that individual.

Unless your customer simply dislikes your product or service, the only resistance to your request you are likely to encounter is an unwillingness to sit down and think of something to say. This is easy to overcome. Proactively suggest the kind of praise you would like to hear: "I know that you are extremely busy, so I've taken the liberty of jotting down a few good words about our product. Perhaps these will help you frame your own remarks."

Asking for the recommendation or testimonial is straightforward. Call or email the customer from whom you would like a referral. Begin by establishing your relationship with him: "John, we've been doing business together now for nearly five years . . ." From here, make your request: "Because of our long and strong relationship, I'm asking you for a referral (or recommendation, or testimonial)." Next, explain how valuable this favor is to you: "Your recommendation will be of tremendous value to my business because you are so highly respected in the widget community." Finally, make it as easy as possible for your customer: "I know how busy you are, so I've jotted down a few good words about our product or service. Feel free to use them." Be certain to close by providing the necessary names and addresses.

EXAMPLES

Phone Call

Mack, hi! I've been approached by Pete Matthews, who, I understand, is a good friend and professional colleague of yours. He's asked me to bid on a new <project>. I don't mind telling you how excited I am about it, and to get myself the best shot at landing the business, I would really appreciate your permission to use your name as a reference. I know it will carry a lot of weight with Pete.

Can I give your name as a reference?

Email

Jane, I'm hoping you can help me. I understand you are a business associate of Howard Morris at Acme Inc. I would really like to connect with him and show him our line of widgets. Could you, please, put in a good word for us? We've worked together so long, and I've sold you so many widgets over the years that I feel if you just tell Mr. Morris about the product features and benefits that have kept you coming back to us all these years, he will become a customer, too. What I'm particularly interested in you highlighting are the following: <list>. And please don't forget to say something about our Super Service Plan, too.

I would be very grateful, Jane, and I feel good about asking you because I know that Howard Morris will be totally satisfied by what we have to offer—just as you are.

Another Email

Ed! Help me!

Boris Fenwick is currently considering us as a contractor for the electrical work on their new headquarters. It's a project very similar to the one we worked on for you last year. I know you were pleased—because you were kind enough to tell me so—and for that reason it seemed to me a no-brainer to ask you for a testimonial.

Can you call him at 555-555-5555 tomorrow or Wednesday?

It would be particularly effective if you could make the following points: <list points>. But, of course, feel free to tell him whatever you want him to know.

Your positive word of mouth will mean the world to us, Boris. Thanks.

WORDS AND PHRASES TO USE

A dynamo

A real go-getter

Able to anticipate and respond
    quickly to problems

Able to inspire others

Able to take control

Absolute commitment

All the necessary skills

Be inspired

Can be counted on

Clear-thinking

Commitment

Dynamic

Enhance your prestige

Experience

Extra-mile service

Follow-up

Gets more done

Gets your needs met

Goal-oriented

Great value

Helps you manage difficult
    change

High-powered

In-depth
Inspiring
Integrity
Long and productive relationship
Meets and exceeds
Meets every challenge
No compromise
Problem solver
Promotes
Quality
Ready to pitch in
Relationship

Satisfaction
Saves you money/time
Superb
Team player
The right choice
Total satisfaction
Works overtime and then some
Your judgment
Your opinion is so highly valued
Your standing in the business
    community

WORDS AND PHRASES TO AVOID

Big, big, big favor
Bother
Desperate
Don't let me down
I hate to ask
I know this is a pain
I'm depending on you
I'm desperate
If it's not too much trouble
If you can
Let me apologize in advance
Little favor

Major favor to ask
Need you to
Put in a good word
Quick favor
Sorry to bother you
Urgent
When you get a chance
Won't take you any time
You owe me
You're my last chance
You've got to help me

CHAPTER 8

Sell a Retail Customer

This chapter is about what most people would call the "casual" or "routine" sales situation. Those are dangerous words, because they imply that it is okay to be unprepared to make a sale. Well, forget that implication. If your business is selling—and *all* of us have to be selling at least *some* of the time—you should always be prepared to sell. Nevertheless, not every sales encounter calls for, is conducive to, or even permits, full and formal preparation. Person-to-person retail sales, the kind that happen every day, are an example of a sales scenario that calls for flexibility and spontaneity—though, let's face it, it all works much better when built on a platform of knowledge and preparation.

PICK UP THE PHONE

You can use the telephone in two ways to make sales. Chapters 9 through 12 in this section of the book focus mainly on prepared or scripted solicitations. These are usually the most practical method for conducting full-scale sales and promotional campaigns. If the script is well written and, equally important, well delivered, the approach is not only practical, but effective as well. But not every solicitation requires a prepared script. Sometimes, opportunity presents itself, as when a prospect or established customer calls you. At other times, the moment just "feels right" for you to make a few phone calls.

Prepare to Be Spontaneous

Few abilities are more admired in business than the faculty of thinking on your feet. Maybe you believe that this is a talent you either have or don't have. To a degree this is, in fact, the case, but the most successful sales professionals work diligently on their "spontaneity," and it is a skill that can quite feasibly be acquired. The most important requisite is full knowledge of and thorough familiarity with the products and services that you are selling. You can't launch into a "spontaneous" sales presentation without knowing what you are selling. The second requisite is enthusiasm for the merchandise.

The third prerequisite isn't absolutely required, but it certainly helps. Consider preparing crib sheets, quick-fact sheets, cue cards—or whatever else you want to call them—that list the most important sales points pertaining to the merchandise or services you offer. Keep these handy by the phone. You might prepare your fact sheets as documents on your computer. If you do, give each sheet a short, easy, relevant title and save them all to relevant folders, so that you can get them up on your screen quickly. For example, your crib sheet for "Model 123" should be Model 123.docx, and it should be saved to a folder such as "2012 Fall Widgets." If you are more comfortable with old-school methods, consider preparing a loose-leaf binder, with tabs, arranged alphabetically or with the hottest products up front. However you prepare your fact lists, your objective is to select a method that conveys to the customer on the other end of the phone not only that your knowledge of your products and services is thorough, but that you yourself are so completely sold on the merchandise that you have the key data at the very top of your mind.

Your "spontaneous" fact sheets should be sufficiently comprehensive to inform and hook the prospect. Don't risk boring him with details he doesn't need to hear. Distill the selling points for each item to their essentials. If the customer expresses interest in knowing more, you can always ask him to wait a moment while you look up a full spec sheet. Not only will your customer not mind waiting a moment or two, he will appreciate the effort you are making to serve him.

Have a Structure in Mind

A truly spontaneous call has only the structure of the moment. A prepared "spontaneous" call, however, should be controlled by a rough outline you keep in your mind. It works like this:

1. Get attention.
2. Identify a need.
3. Show that you can fill this need.
4. Persuade the prospect to buy.
5. Prompt the prospect to take action.

WARM IT UP

In Chapter 2, we talked about the difference between cold calls and warm calls. True cold calls are typically not very productive. Even when you decide to make some "casual" sales calls—calls that don't follow a hot lead or that are not made in specific response to a customer's call—it is best to draw up beforehand a quick call list of established customers or others you have some reason to believe will be interested in your product or service. So, as you sit down to your calls, have on hand a short list of potentially interested customers as well as your fact sheets. Your objective is to be able to answer the question "Why should I be interested in this merchandise?" and to answer it even if it is not asked.

EXAMPLES

Casual "Warm" Call

YOU: Hello, Mr. Johnson, this is Pat Perkins of Modern Product. You may recall that we spoke at the trade show last March. At the time, you mentioned that you were interested in widgets. Well, we have just acquired a terrific new widget, which I think you would like to know about, and we are offering it at a very special introductory price. Would you like to hear more?

PROSPECT: Yes.

YOU: Splendid! Let me tell you a little about it. <Hit main points from fact sheet; include key features and key benefits—what the product will *do* for the customer. Do *not* mention the price until your prospect asks about it.>

PROSPECT: And the price?

YOU: Normally, these will sell for $XXX, with the popular options package adding $XX. *Our* introductory price, *including* the popular options package, is just $XX. Now, that introductory pricing period ends soon, so, if you are interested, well, now is the time.

Casual Call Based on Customer Referral

As we've said repeatedly in this book, your best prospects are current customers. Satisfied current customers are also your best sales prospectors. No form of advertising outperforms word of mouth. When a current customer furnishes you with a lead to new business, follow it. If your informant tells you that someone wants the product and is ready to buy *now*, you have a hot lead. More often, however, the referral will be an expression of *possible* interest, and so you are presented with a setup for a "warm" call bolstered by the personal connection that a current customer gave you the name of a prospective customer. That is, you and the prospect know someone in common. Begin your "spontaneous" sales call by invoking that relationship:

YOU: Hello, Ms. Smith. This is Max Perkins from Pinnacle Goods. I was just talking to a friend of yours, who is also a longtime customer of mine, Mary Lou Norton. She mentioned this morning that you are somebody who would want to hear from me about a solution we offer to your <identify problem or need>. Mary Lou said you have been looking for a solution, but that so far you haven't found anything suitable. Do I understand the situation correctly?

PROSPECT: You do.

YOU: Well, then, I *am* glad that Mary Lou put me in touch with you. Pinnacle has a brand-new product that I believe will give you exactly what you want. What's more, since I know you have been shopping around for a while, I know you will find our prices very, very competitive. Can I tell you more?

PROSPECT: Yes, I'm interested. I have been looking for a long time now.

YOU: Well, this may just be the end of your search. <Tick off the highlights from your fact sheet.> Now, if you're eager to get this system up and running, I can have an installer out to you before the end of the week.

Call Based on Quick-and-Dirty Market "Research"

Not all market research needs to be thorough, formal—and costly. Let's say you happen to hear that Juan Martinez is in the market for a particular product you stock. This is market research. *Act* on the information. Or, you're talking to your outside IT service tech, who tells you that he's just made his umpteenth service call to Modern Design. "It's about time they look into replacing their servers," he says. You've got servers to sell, and you've just been provided with some market research. Sell.

Hello, Mr. Samuels. My name is Jane Darling, and I own Darling Widgets. I'd like to offer you some information on our new line, which includes three widgets that I believe would suit your particular needs perfectly. They offer <list relevant features/benefits>. Am I correct in assuming that this is what you need?

If the response is positive, use your fact sheet to hit the high points in greater detail. Then close the sale by moving the prospect to action:

I understand if you are anxious to upgrade. I can come right out to your plant as early as this afternoon, if you like.

RESPONDING TO TELEPHONE INQUIRES

A prospect who calls to inquire about a product may tell you—and may even believe—that he is calling "only to get some information, not to buy." Even if mere information is the only thing the caller (believes he) seeks, don't limit yourself to supplying nothing more than information. Instead, respond to what is almost certainly the underlying motive of the call. He wants to *buy* something.

Greet the caller. Give your name and your company name, then immediately focus the call with "How may I help you?" The phrase is not "May I help you?" or "What can I do for you?" The phrase of choice is *"How may I help you?"* It gently but firmly prompts your caller to define her request in a full sentence, creating precision that ultimately saves both of you time and that sets up a positive context in which the chances for misunderstanding are minimized from the outset.

In many cases, "How may I help you?" will elicit a response like "I'm looking for such-and-such a product." This is a buy signal. Act on it by assuring the caller that she has come to the right place: "I can certainly help you with that," then continue:

> We offer a wide variety of <products>. Let me ask you a few questions to get us to precisely what's right for you.

What you ask depends on what you are selling. As with the fact sheet, consider preparing a list of basic questions to have on hand. Ask whatever is necessary to define the caller's wants and needs. Once you understand these, make your recommendations:

> YOU: Okay. I understand. Based on what you've told me, I suggest that you consider either <product 1> or <product 2>. Both will satisfy your requirements, but <product 1> will also <list additional functions>. Are those additional features important to you?
>
> CALLER: Depends on what they cost.
>
> YOU: The price of <product 1> is $XX, compared with $XX for <product 2>. You, of course, will make the choice as to what value the additional features of <product 1> have *for you*. If you do want <additional functions>, the higher price is actually quite cost-effective.

If the caller hesitates, try to elicit action: "May I take your order for <product 1> or <product 2>?" If this produces more doubt and delay, ask how you might help her decide: "Is there any more information I might supply to help you make your choice?" Note that *choice* is preferable to the word *decision*, which conveys pressure, even compulsion. *Choice*, in contrast, is about empowerment and freedom. It puts the action in a positive context.

STRATEGIES FOR FOCUSING PROSPECTS

Shoppers invariably say they love stores that offer a wide variety and many choices. Nevertheless, many prospective customers become confused, frustrated, overwhelmed, and even paralyzed by an abundance of choice. If the effort of deciding becomes too stressful for your caller, you may lose a sale. It is, after all, easy to hang up a phone.

When a prospect is uncertain or unclear about his needs or has difficulty choosing among a wide range of variations, you have several choices:

1. You can just sell the caller *something*, anything.
2. You can offer to send a catalog and ask him to call back later.
3. You can bombard the caller with questions until he loses all interest in buying the item.
4. You can ask a select few questions that focus on matching needs with features and benefits.

Alternative 4 is obviously the most productive means of closing the sale.

Approach the process not as a salesperson desperate for a sale, but as a counselor, as one who is willing to work with the customer to ensure that her needs are met and met optimally. The truly successful sales scenario is one in which the customer perceives the selling process itself as value added to the purchase. Begin by asking about the intended use. Once this area has been addressed, turn to cost. Preface your questions with a gentle *helping* remark: "Let's take just a few moments to work through your requirements together," or "Take a few moments to work with me so that we can connect you with just the right product."

The key here is patience. If the customer perceives you as impatient, he will not only become anxious, but become impatient as well. Hold somewhere in a corner of your mind the following motto: *The customer is not an interruption of your business day; the customer is the reason for your business day.*

Commit to an investment of whatever time is necessary, but do not make the mistake of trying to persuade the customer that he *needs* this or that product. Instead, invest time leading him through the process of choice. If you keep the process interactive, your customer will not feel that his time is being wasted, but, rather, he will be grateful to you for devoting so much time to his needs. Furthermore, understand that the more time both parties invest in the negotiation, the more likely it is that it will end in a good sale.

OVERCOMING RESISTANCE

In Chapter 5, we discussed strategies and tactics for overcoming objections. Review them, but also understand that it may be more difficult for you to answer objections when they are made in the course of a "casual" or "spontaneous" call. You may not be fully prepared to deal with them, and you may even be less willing to devote the energy, time, and effort required. True, if the customer tells you flatly that she is not interested in what you have to offer, cease and desist, but do not end the call abruptly. Instead, sign off with something like "I understand. Thanks very much for your time, and I hope you'll keep us in mind should your needs change." Bear in mind that most resistance is not so absolute and final. Objections are usually less the product of a decision not to buy than a request for your help in making a buying decision. When you sense that the resistance is built on "I don't know" or "I'm not sure" rather than "I really do not want to buy," offer your guidance.

Offer Education

Consider the following expressions of resistance:

> "Isn't that terribly expensive?"
> "The cost would be prohibitive."

"I've heard those things don't work very well."

"Well, I've always used such and such."

Don't argue, and certainly do not deny the validity of the customer's feelings, perceptions, preconceptions, preferences, or prejudices. Instead, simply show her alternatives:

PROSPECT: It's just too expensive for me.

YOU: I agree that <product> requires a substantial investment. However, our experience has shown that the investment pays off because the <product> is so cost-effective. On average, you will save $XX per year in energy costs—not to mention time saved. As the old saying goes, it pays for itself. We also offer in-house financing. So the outlay is not as formidable as it may seem.

The most effective way to overcome resistance is to show—not tell—your prospect how to overcome it. If you and your prospect encounter an obstacle, your task is to point the way around it.

Dealing with Postponement

Listen for any of the following:

"Can you call me about it later?"

"I'm too busy to think about it now."

"I'm not ready to buy yet."

Postponement cannot be overcome by nagging, pleading, goading, or heavy-handed persuasion. What the prospect is telling you is that he is *burdened* by uncertainty and indecision. Your most helpful move, therefore, is to take on some of the burden yourself. Ask:

"What can I do to help you make your choice?"

"What additional information will help you move on to the next step?"

"How can I help you define your options?"

Most sales professionals reach a point in their pitch when they wish *they* could get some help. Well, this is precisely how a lot of customers feel when they are trying to make a purchasing decision. Empathize with them. If *you* don't offer your prospect assistance, who will?

WORDS AND PHRASES TO USE

Alternative

Answer to your needs

Available in several finishes

Benefit

Breakthrough

Choice/Choose

Choose one that fits your
    individual need

Clear choice

Compare your choices

Count on us

Desirable

Discriminating

Distinctive

Easy

Faster order turnaround

Fits any taste or budget

For the future

Free

Free next-day delivery

Full service

Good reason

Great fit

Highly desirable

Ideal choice

If you need it, we have it

Immediate

Indulge yourself

Just tell us when you need it

Large capacity

Let me answer

Let me help

Luxury of choices

Make up your own mind

Most desirable/requested/wanted

Now in stock

Now it's your turn

Opportunity

Option

Order now for best selection

Perfect fit

Popular

Problem solver

Prove

Ready for delivery

Rely on us

See

Smart

Smartest choice you'll ever make

Solves the issue

Such possibilities!

Superior

Taste

Tell me about it

Test

The adventure begins here

The better/best choice

The selection you deserve

The superior choice

Touch

Trustworthy

Unequaled opportunity

Value

Wanted

We have the right one to suit your needs

We service what we sell

We ship straight from the warehouse

Will work

Win

Wise

You have choices in life

Your one-stop shop

WORDS AND PHRASES TO AVOID

Absolutely last chance

As is

Buy now

Cheap

Contract

Decide

Decision

Don't wimp out

Last chance

Lose out

Must decide

Never another chance

No choice

Opportunity of a lifetime

Take a chance

Take the plunge

Urge you to decide

What have you got to lose?

You assume all responsibility

CHAPTER 9

Sell a Purchasing Manager

A purchasing manager is anyone whose job is buying supplies and equipment for an organization. In larger enterprises, "purchasing manager" (PM) is a full-time specialty. In many smaller firms, office managers, controllers, and others frequently double as purchasing managers. In both cases, sales personnel have a natural tendency to assume that when they are working with a PM, they are dealing with professional buyers who have no personal agenda. It is also widely assumed that PMs are ruthless price buyers, that they regard most of what they purchase as nothing more than a commodity (one brand is much like another), and that all they really care about is price.

To some degree, these assumptions are accurate. Purchasing managers are, in fact, customers who make buying decisions about products and services they don't personally use. In this, they are significantly different from retail customers or from end users in a business context. It is also true that the PM's performance is generally judged by how well she meets—or even undercuts—her budget targets. Nevertheless, purchasing managers are not price-driven automatons. They are people, dealing with pressures and juggling sometimes conflicting needs and wants. Always remember, no business ever does business with another business. People in business do business with other people in business. Do not try to sell to a purchasing manager without understanding the *full* human extent of what he needs and he wants. It all goes well beyond prices and specs on a purchase order.

BE THE ANSWER, RECRUIT AN ALLY

Whatever specifications a PM wants your product or service to meet, whatever cost targets he is trying to meet, all PMs have at least one need and many have *two* conflicting needs.

1. Purchasing managers are support staff. They understand that they are paid to perform a specific and particular task, which is representing the company in making purchasing decisions.

Straightforward as this may seem, the job often involves a basic problem. The PM is, in effect, an intermediary, often asked to make buying decisions about merchandise she may not fully understand from the perspective of the end user. She may lack the technical background needed to evaluate all of the products she is assigned to buy. This means that the typical PM must frequently shuttle between the sales rep—you—and the end users in her own organization. The bind here is that the sales manager may be ill-equipped to make decisions for which she must nevertheless accept full responsibility and, if things go wrong, all the blame.

2. In addition to the universal need to do a specific job (that entails pressures others don't always understand), many purchasing managers feel underappreciated within their organization and therefore are chronically frustrated.

Many PMs want to get the same recognition, respect, rewards, and opportunities for advancement that "line" personnel—"creative" people, upper-level executives, marketers, and the like—enjoy, yet they are generally classified as "support," "back-office," "operations," or "staff" personnel. Let's face it, this attitude is not paranoia. The fact is that, in most corporate cultures, there is an undeniable bias in favor of "line" or "front-office" people.

Sales and Production are top-of-mind departments, whereas Purchasing, like Human Resources and Accounting, is relegated to a corner of the corporate consciousness. If purchasing managers often resent this situation, they do so with good reason, since they themselves may be resented by "line" personnel, who see them as having secure, insulated jobs in the rear echelon, out of the line of fire. They may well be regarded as also-rans rather than as the best and the brightest; competent, perhaps, but hardly brilliant. As the late comic Rodney Dangerfield used to say of himself, they "don't get no respect."

To maximize your chances not only of making a particular sale, but of cultivating a purchasing manager as a reliable source of ongoing sales, pitch yourself and your company as what every PM urgently, desperately needs: problem solvers.

With respect to the first issue—the problem *all* purchasing managers have—begin by doing your best to present your offering as a high value, with emphasis on giving the best possible price. This said, recognize that even though most purchasing managers *say* price trumps all other considerations, about two-thirds of them report that they routinely adjust specs and/or calculations so that they can award purchase orders to providers they most favor and are most comfortable with. Relationships are, therefore, important. In fact, some two-thirds of the time, relationships outweigh considerations of price.

Also be aware that on-time delivery frequently trumps price as the most important determining factor in the purchase decision. Price is important, but if the product or service does not arrive when and where it is required, the purchasing manager has failed outright, no matter what price he has managed to negotiate.

The Brooks Group, a corporate sales-training consulting firm, argues persuasively that, among PMs, value often supersedes price (www.brooksgroup .com/articles/selling-to-purchasing-managers.htm). Depending on the product, such considerations as useful product life, anticipated benefits, compatibility, and upgrade ability (to prevent obsolescence) are significant issues of cost-effectiveness that a PM can bring to his bosses.

The sales lesson here is never to swallow whole the old price-is-king stereotype, but to instead create what the sales professional attempts to create with each and every customer: productive rapport. With respect to the universal issue, this means always projecting sincerity, integrity, and reliability. Add to these qualities an attitude that addresses the second set of issues by communicating with empathy. Give the PM what her colleagues rarely give her. Make her feel important, respected, and appreciated.

Understand what it means to be dealing with an intermediary. If you are aware that the purchasing manager is not technically savvy and does not have the full technical understanding of an end user, avoid making an overly technical pitch, and make it clear that you welcome his questions: "No question is too complicated—or too easy." When you give an answer, be sure to respond on the purchasing manager's level, not that of the end user. Check to make sure that you are getting through: "Did I answer your question clearly and fully?"

The nutshell message to deliver is this:

> "I am confident that I understand what you want and need. You want solutions that you can rely on, including on-time delivery and installation. You want the best price. But, even more, you want the most cost-effective value. You want to satisfy the techies in Production, but you don't need me to dump a heap of specs on you. The bottom line? You want to make a buying decision that will clearly and unmistakably contribute to your company's success. Am I understanding you correctly?"

SELL THE GOODS, SELL THE ORGANIZATION

You and the PM are fortunate in one respect. The moment you meet each other, you can count on having at least one goal in common. Neither of you wants just a single sale. What you both want is to build a relationship. You want reliable repeat business. The PM wants a reliable supplier, who can deliver solutions quickly, dependably, and at a good price over and over again. Auditioning new suppliers is a time-consuming effort, fraught with risk. The PM knows she is much better off having a tested, reliable vendor always on tap. Therefore, you need to sell your product or service as well as yourself and your organization.

Selling the Merchandise

If you are selling a utilitarian product or service—the nature of much B2B merchandise—you will be tempted to put all the emphasis in your presentation on features: what the product does, what it's made out of, what it costs to operate, and so on. Make no mistake, these are important. But even more important when you are dealing with someone other than the end user is to recognize that your immediate prospect almost certainly feels self-conscious about the limitations of his technical knowledge. For this reason, put most of your energy and time into presenting the benefits of your merchandise, especially the two benefits that are certainly of most concern to the purchasing manager: *It will solve his problems. It will keep him from making a mistake.* This can be broken down further. Consider delivering these messages:

- It will do the job.
- It is cost-effective.
- It is reliable.
- It will be delivered and installed correctly and on time.
- You are offering the best possible price.
- It will get the purchasing manager recognized for what he is: a hero.

Making these points requires that you persuade the purchasing manager that your product or service is "easy to understand." In fact, use that phrase—*easy to understand*—and embellish it with:

Technically sophisticated, but a breeze to operate
Requires no technical training
Not a challenge to operate or maintain
Our advanced technology is tested technology
It is a safe, solid investment

EXAMPLE

"Mark, what I need to emphasize is that this machine is so advanced that it is actually easy to understand and easy to operate day in and day out.

We have solved all the technical challenges. There is nothing for you to figure out or to do. The technology, though cutting edge, is highly tested, and you will be making a safe and solid investment for the people in your company. They will be grateful to you for it."

Selling the Organization

We all know that many people have a kneejerk response to the very word *salesman*. For them, it automatically conjures up images of shallowness and deception. We might assume that purchasing managers, who deal with sales-people every day and for whom sales professionals are, in effect, business partners, would be free from such negative stereotypes. In some instances, this is probably the case; however, it is also true that because the future of the purchasing manager's job depends so heavily on dealing with sales profes-sionals, she may well be even more fearful and suspicious of their character and motives. Subject as they are to a great deal of pressure and very little gratitude, purchasing managers are particularly vulnerable to a cynical point of view where the motives of salespeople are concerned. The result is that when you call on a purchasing manager, even before you utter word one, there is a good possibility the she already regards you as insincere, lacking in integrity, and concerned only with making a sale. And, let's admit it, a lot of salespeople are manipulative and insincere. Most customers don't have to reach too far back in memory to recall a bad sales experience.

When you sell directly to owners and CEOs, your sincerity is less impor-tant than your product. The CEO feels powerful. She answers, perhaps, to a board of directors, but to no one else. In contrast, the purchasing manager is in the difficult position of having to make a decision and take responsibility for that decision; yet, often, he lacks the technical knowledge required to make the decision, and he does not have the power to survive the conse-quences of a really bad decision. Understandably, this situation strikes fear in the heart of many a PM, and for that reason, your integrity and sincerity are very important to him. He relies on your word. In fact, it may be the only thing he can rely on.

This makes a significant demand on you, but, of course, it also offers you a great opportunity. You are put in the position of recruiting the PM as an ally and a champion, a genuine partner in success—yours and his. What is required from you is patience coupled with a nurturing, understanding, empathetic tone:

1. Avoid coming across as "all business." Be a person.
2. Never show more interest in selling your merchandise than in the customer. Make it clear that your primary objective is to make him look like a hero. The benefit you are selling is not a widget. The benefit is the PM's ultimate success.
3. Because the PM is *not* the end user, you will probably feel a strong urge to school her on the technical details of your merchandise. Usually, going the extra mile to educate a customer is a good thing. But not in this case. Your objective is to present the product as something that is very easy to understand. By all means, convey its principal benefits; that is, make sure the PM knows that it works and that it is a good value. Do not, however, try to conduct an impromptu seminar on its technical features. *You* may be *selling* a very sophisticated piece of technology, but what the *PM* wants to *buy* is a solution to her problems. End of story. Period. Her objective is not to become a technical expert, but merely to avoid blundering. Build confidence. Offer reassurance. Make her feel comfortable with the decision you are guiding her toward.

Don't just sell your own integrity, sincerity, empathy, and commitment. Present yourself as a representative of your company's values. In fact, don't call your company your "company." Whenever possible, refer instead to your "colleagues," "folks," "people," and "team." Make it clear that you see yourself as part of a team of *human beings* who are dealing with another team of *human beings*—and, most immediately, with a single human being for whom you feel appreciation, respect, and professional admiration.

EXAMPLE

"Mark, let me say something about our team. Everyone on it is focused on creating high-tech excellence so that *you* don't have to sweat the technical details. Not ever. What we sell works. It works the first time and every time. Feel free to call me or our support people if you ever have a question. We're eager to help you understand and get the most out of the equipment, but just understand that we are a lot more interested in our customers and in their needs, than we are in the technology of what we sell. If you succeed, we all look good—and we all stay in business together."

THE VALUE PROPOSITION

Just as you don't want to bury a purchasing manager in technical language he neither understands nor really wants to understand, avoid snowing yourself under a pile of technology. If you love what you sell, it may actually be difficult for you to break the habit of waxing poetic about bits, bytes, horsepower, rotors, pneumatics, whatever. But try to remember: *You* are not the customer. Focus not on what intrigues or impresses you, but on what you know to be the PM's needs. The two primary benefits she wants are (1) to be seen as having done her job well (she has purchased something that works, that was delivered on time, and that represents a good value) and (2) not to make a mistake. In fact, the PM's job is such that she is far more likely to be condemned for failure than praised for good performance. This being the unhappy case, the second benefit actually outweighs the first.

Your marching orders are therefore clear. Sell the benefit of certainty and confidence. Sell the benefit of *avoiding* error. Let your customer know that, with you, your team, and your product behind him, he is invulnerable and all will be well. Everything will come together like clockwork. Satisfaction will be universal and total throughout his company. There will be no drama, no crisis, no crying, no finger-pointing. He can sleep well at night, in the full assurance and confidence that he has made the best possible decision.

EXAMPLE

"Mark, our machine works. It just works. And that means things will hum along smoothly for you and your people. We guarantee that, of course. But you also have my word that when you deal with our team, all the decisions you make will be solid and sure. Count on it."

AND YES—PRICE

As critically important as it to bond with the purchasing manager by presenting yourself, your firm, and your product as the solution to all of her problems, never forget that one of those problems does indeed concern price. The PM knows that price is the first thing her bosses will look at. Sometimes (she also knows) it will be the *only* thing they look at. Understand that, just as the purchasing manager is not the end user, she also personally cares very little about price. What she *does* care very much about is the people in her firm's Finance Department, for whom price is the *only* thing that matters.

Begin, therefore, by offering the best price you possibly can. There is no substitute for this as a mover of sales. If your price is lower than your competitors', great. If, however, it is comparable, let alone higher, you must be able to present all of your product's benefits so compellingly that they clearly come across as benefits obviously worth the "extra" cost.

EXAMPLE

"You and I aren't interested in playing games with each other, right? The price I've quoted is the very best we offer. The numbers are the numbers, and, clearly, our competitor's number *is* lower. Just be aware that both their number and ours are directly related to the benefits you will receive. When you compare our reliability with theirs, our reputation, the ratings of our technology, and our team's record for reliability, I know you will agree that our nominally higher number is more than justified by the benefits you and your company will enjoy. The price is easy to justify because it is *more* than justified by those benefits."

WORDS AND PHRASES TO USE

A dose of tranquility	Be more in control
A superior solution	Benefits
Absolute confidence	Built for the future
An expert solution	Clear winner
Be a winner	Cool and confident

Count on me/us
Credit you deserve
Customer-centered
Design wizardry
Easy to install/operate/program
Effective solution
Enjoy control
Everyone will be satisfied
Feel more in control
For the future
Free technical support/upgrade
  program
Has a positive impact
High value
Ideal for you
It just works
Just what you need
Look no further
No drama/problems/second-
  guessing/stress/trouble
Non-technical
One-stop shop
Overcome self-doubt
People business
Problem solvers
Quickly and quietly

Reduces stress
Safe and solid
Simple
Sincere
Solution
Solve problems
Straightforward
Take control
Takes just minutes
Team
Technology so simple you won't
  even know it's there
This is the one
This is the right decision
Tomorrow's technology today
Trouble-free
Value
We are people, and we are more
  interested in our customers
  than in what we're selling
We're people who aren't obsessed
  with the technical details of
  our products
We're the one
We've got the answer
What you've been looking for

WORDS AND PHRASES TO AVOID

Better be careful
I can't take the time to explain it
I'm no expert
I'm pretty sure you've made the
  right decision
It's complicated

Just take my word for it
Leave that to the experts
Nobody understands this stuff,
  believe me
The price is the price, I'm afraid
There is a learning curve

There's a lot to learn

This requires considerable training

We'll try to squeeze you in

You can't expect something for nothing

You can't expect to be up and running overnight

You don't want to get burned

You don't want to make a mistake

You wouldn't understand

CHAPTER 10

Sell a Corporate Executive

When you sell to a corporate executive, you sell to an individual who either has—or feels she has—an ownership stake in her firm. In contrast to the purchasing manager (Chapter 9), the executive tends to make purchasing decisions based on her own sense of the company's image and core strategy. That is, each major purchase is at least to some degree an element of strategy and vision. Moreover, whereas the purchasing manager is, in effect, merely an agent, making purchases on behalf of others (namely, his bosses or the heads of other departments), the executive typically approaches each purchase personally. Each system, piece of equipment, office machine, item of furniture, or fixture she chooses is, for her, an expression of leadership and planning. If the purchase proves productive and satisfying to her and her employees, as well as to her superiors and/or investors, she will believe that her business acumen and strategic wisdom have been vindicated, demonstrated, and fairly exhibited. If, however, the purchase proves unsatisfactory—or even worse, disastrous—she may well feel that her employees, colleagues, bosses, investors, and any other stakeholders now have unwelcome evidence of her failure. Although the executive customer enjoys more power and authority than a purchasing manager, she, like him, is subject to substantial pressures and anxieties. The sales professional who understands these and creates empathy based on that understanding will always have the edge on other vendors.

SELL A CEO

The biggest difference between selling to a CEO or other C-level executive and those at lower levels in a corporation is the need to appreciate that these leaders take an intense, immediate, personal, and unique interest in hard numbers and short-term performance—the quarterly report—combined with a long-term vision for their enterprise. Both halves of this bifurcated focus carry with them their own needs, wants, concerns, and anxieties, but the most important consideration of all is strategic vision. In selling to the purchasing manager, you have some fairly straightforward needs to address. In selling to the C-level executive, however, you must not only address these, but also direct the sales conversation toward answering the question that is always lurking in the mind of any enterprise leader: *Where will I take my company next?*

Most sales professionals are eager to zero in on specific needs, so that they can present their merchandise as the best means of addressing those needs. Yet when you sell to C-level executives, focusing on immediate, obvious needs is not sufficient to create a compelling personal bond between you and the prospect. While the executive may be quite interested in getting an immediate job done, she is also accustomed to delegating most immediate needs to subordinates. Her highest-priority concern is visionary and strategic. Her concentration is ultimately on the future of the company she leads. Sell product features to address the immediate needs—"You need the following. This is what I have that meets those needs."—but sell product benefits to address the big picture, the long-term vision: "I understand your vision for this company. I appreciate where you are going. Now, let me show you how our product (or service) will help get you there."

Ask questions that define short-term needs, and ask questions that help you to understand the executive's long-term vision. Once you have answers to the issues in both of these dimensions, you can help the executive make the connections between immediate needs and long-term vision by showing how your product links the one to the other.

Guide the executive toward making the buy decision by inviting her to envision what the future will be like with your product.

> "What will it be like—how much more will you accomplish—when we deliver and install the new servers? We've gone over the numbers, but the real impact is not in dollars, but in the liberation of your imagination and vision. What will it feel like not to be chronically constrained by inadequate storage and limited bandwidth? What will you be able to accomplish? How will this free your creative vision?"

One of the great myths about corporate leaders is that they're all mind and no heart—that a business pro never lets herself get emotional. On the contrary, most people who have ascended to the C-level suite got there on a combination of their competence, vision, and passion. Appeal to the vision. Stir the passion. In short, guide the executive a step beyond "What do you need?" and toward "Where are you going? How can we work together to get you there?"

SELLING THE CFO OR THE FINANCIALLY FOCUSED CEO

The objective of leading the executive from immediate need to ultimate vision is twofold. First, it is where the executive *most* wants to be. Take him there, and he will know that you "get it," that you understand the scope of his ambitions for his company. Second, by demonstrating your understanding and appreciation of his vision, you reserve a place for yourself and your company in the customer's long-term plans. Remember, a good salesperson makes a sale. A great salesperson creates a customer—the source of many sales over many years.

Just don't get lost in someone else's vision. Your goal is to ground your presentation in present needs, but with an eye toward the future. Nowhere is this more important than when you present to a financially focused CEO or a chief financial officer (CFO). Your objective here is to sell solidity and prudence as a basis of vision. Bond with this prospect through the language of stability and reality. Emphasize such product benefits as—

Creates a solid foundation.
Will reward every stakeholder.
You will be assured that you have the right standards in place.
We help you manage the risks while you envision the rewards.

EXAMPLE

Vendor of Strategic Modeling Software

"You've created a great career and a great company. You have a vision for future growth. What you need for the present is strategic modeling software that identifies all the unknowns and intangibles and makes them both known and tangible. I appreciate what you want. You want to know, not to guess—because knowing is always better than guessing.

"So with all that you have achieved and all that you plan to achieve in the future, what you need is modeling tools that you can rely on and that don't introduce additional risk into an inherently risky business. By contributing to your process certain key standards—transparent and thoroughly defined—we end your dependence on guesswork.

"Just imagine what it will feel like to shed nagging doubts about fudged figures and other guesswork. You won't have to feel that you are groping in the dark with a dim flashlight. And, best of all, we'll back you all the way—with support, advice, and continual upgrades that will keep you on the cutting edge."

WORDS AND PHRASES TO USE

A sound/tested business model
Advance your vision while protecting the means of its fulfillment
Balanced
Control risk
Credibility
Designed with finance and operations in mind

Does exactly what needs to
   be done

Enlarge the margin between you
   and risk

Enlightened

Evolutionary rather than
   revolutionary

Exquisitely balanced

Firm grasp on reality

Free of drama

Growth without disruption

Imagination by the numbers

Incorporates industry best
   practices

Keeps you centered/your thinking
   centered

Knowing beats guessing any day
   of the week

Logistically sound

Major career investment

Manage risk

Median solution

Minimize risk

Moderate

No controversy

No disruption

Nobody will argue about it

No-nonsense

Play offense with your
   reputation

Progress without disruption

Protect what's been built/your
   brand while advancing it/your
   vision

Prudent

Return on investment

Seamless transition

Spread the risk

Stable

Turnkey but controllable

Undemanding

Why rely on guesswork?

WORDS AND PHRASES TO AVOID

Ambitious

Educated guess

Guesstimate

I believe it will work

I think it should

Impulse

Major change

Matchless ROI

Never been done

No reward without substantial risk

Once-in-a-lifetime return on
   investment

Pioneering

Pure imagination

Shot in the dark

Spontaneous

Super ambitious

Take a flier/a stab/the risk

This will sure shake
   things up

SELLING THE CTO OR
THE TECHNOLOGY-FOCUSED CEO

It used to be that a sales professional could confidently make some easy as-sumptions about any business leader with a "technology" background. Such individuals were typically trained as engineers, and that meant you had to sell them on what they already valued: the benefits of stability, the elimina-tion of "surprises," the replacement of guesswork with hard numbers, and a promise of progress and evolution, but with stepwise control. The watchword was *fail-safe*.

Today, the situation is more complicated. The tech-focused CEO still wants the solidity of science and engineering, but he also favors produc-tive predictability over status-quo certainty, and he typically puts concepts, creativity, innovation, and outside-the-box thinking in the forefront of all other considerations. If you had to distill to a sentence the single benefit that is of greatest value to the modern tech-oriented CEO or chief technology of-ficer, it would be this: *Give me something entirely new that's worked well in the past.*

Impossible? Not really.

Difficult? Perhaps—but promising delivery of this oxymoronic product, something both innovative *and* proven is mostly a matter of balanced expres-sion and a presentation founded on a basic appreciation of engineering. The best engineers have always applied time-tested principles to the creation of innovation. Understand this, give equal weight to the prospect's need for both a solid foundation *and* a soaring new tower, and you will very likely bond productively with the technology-focused CEO or CTO.

Emphasize such benefits as:

Innovative designs based on proven technologies that stabilize and
   energize your work environment.
Cutting-edge technology built on proved principles.
Enhanced productivity with novel applications of time-tested
   approaches.

EXAMPLE

"I'm a salesman who comes out of a technology and engineering culture. So I *get* your organization, and I fully appreciate your vision. You've made a lifetime investment in your career and your company. You are now selling into a marketplace that demands innovation, but you also need to protect what you've built. Well, what we deliver is fail-safe predictability that enables your innovation. Our designs are proved in the real world, yet they are scalable to your ever-evolving needs. They bring industry-standard best practices to your innovative, bold, and bar-raising demands.

"I'm asking you to let us partner with your vision. Wouldn't you like to have the confidence to innovate using tools that have stood the test of time, that have already been used in a dazzling array of applications, and that have been developed by people who understand precisely what you need? It will be a great, liberating, confidence-building feeling. That I can promise you."

WORDS AND PHRASES TO USE

A step beyond
Able to quantify that for you
Add stability
Apply proven designs to
    innovation
Backups
Best practices
Built-in redundancy
Control progress
Customizable
Demonstrated
Dependable
Engineering culture
Established
Evolutionary innovation
Fail-safe

High-value engineering
Industry standard
Introduce innovation
Known
Large install base
Minimizes risk
No guesswork
No stress
One step at a time
Out-of-the-box thinking based on
    time-tested principles
Predictable
Protect what you've built
Proved technology
Quantifiable
Range of applications

Real world

Redundant systems

Reliable

Repeatable

Safe

Safety priority

Scalability/scalable

Stabilized

Super-redundant

Tested

Transparent

Turnkey when you
  want it

Well-known

Wide margin of safety

Without doubt

WORDS AND PHRASES TO AVOID

All new

Bold

Breakthrough

Daring

Estimate

Experimental

Frankly experimental

Guesstimate

Human factor

Ingenious

Intuition

Intuitive design

Inventive

Major change

New, new, new

People-oriented

Pioneering

Pushes the envelope

Revolutionary

Spectacular

State-of-the-art

The latest

The *new* thing

Unprecedented

Untried

SELLING THE MID-LEVEL EXECUTIVE

When you sell to executives below the C-level—so-called mid-level executives—it is very helpful to know whether you are dealing with what we might call a *mainstreamer* or with a real *decision maker*.

Mainstreamers are reluctant to stick their necks out. They value teamwork and safety most highly. Their orientation is far more defensive than aggressive; they are more comfortable playing defense than offense. Often, they strive to insulate themselves. Make no mistake, their objective is not necessarily to maintain the status quo. In fact, most executives, including the mainstreamers, realize that trying to avoid all change is a deceptive strategy that results not in stability and standing still, but in actual regression and backsliding. Nevertheless, the mainstreamers are far more interested in advancing steadily and in baby steps rather than attempting a "great leap forward" breakthrough.

Selling to the mainstreamer calls for messages that convey the capacity of your product or service to support what has already been accomplished. While emphasizing that your offerings are right in line with the direction the company is currently taking, you must avoid implying that it is a departure from what is being done. This is not to say that you should avoid promoting your product or service as a more efficient and more cost-effective way of maintaining the current course. All customers are interested in doing things better. It's just that the mainstreamer wants to do essentially the same things he and his organization are currently doing.

In contrast to mainstreamers, the real decision makers are open to and even eager for new ideas and creative answers to their problems. They are at the edge—and the upper edge at that—of middle management, and they want to be excited by new ideas, solutions, and products so that they, in turn, can excite the C-level just above them, into which they want most earnestly to break. The decision maker sees her job as identifying the next big thing and carrying the information to those just above her. Whereas in approaching the mainstreamer, you sell the benefits of teamwork, consensus, remaining in the mainstream, and gradual, evolutionary improvement rather than breakthroughs, your task in selling to the decision maker is to create the exciting atmosphere of potential for substantial change.

Do Research, Ask Questions, Make Assumptions

As when you prepare for any important sales call, do thorough research on the company and, to the extent that you can, research the executive(s) to whom you will be presenting. Your first stop is the company website. Your second stop should be trade publications (online and in print) that carry stories about the target company and its personnel. Also look for press releases and the investor prospectus, both of which can usually be found online. Your goal is to learn as much as you can about the company to enable you to begin your presentation by focusing on its current position in the in-dustry, the opportunities and challenges it faces, and the strategies its leaders have articulated to exploit the opportunities and meet the challenges.

Just how thoroughly should you prepare? At least thoroughly enough to pass a test on the subject—a test that you yourself administer.

After you present *your* overview of the company, you will want to ask the executive(s) if *your* understanding of *their* company's strategy and goals is accurate. This is not only a good practice from the point of view of creating customer satisfaction by ensuring that you will be directing your efforts ap-propriately, it is enormously flattering to mid-level executives. It shows that you consider them essential to the direction of the company. If the executive you are addressing is a decision maker, this will come to him as catnip. But even if he is not, it will come across as a sign of recognition and respect that will be sincerely appreciated. It may also elicit from the executive a valuable piece of information in response: "Yes, it's an accurate presentation, but I'm not really in on all of the C-level decisions." Now you know that you are deal-ing with a mainstreamer and not a decision maker.

By the way, if you plan to illustrate your presentation with slides, make sure to feature the company's logo. Some presenters go as far as to include a picture of corporate headquarters or a production plant as well. This degree of customization and identification with the prospect costs you nothing, yet makes an effective statement about your interest in the target firm.

Before you go into the next part of your presentation—your company and its offerings—ask questions that extend your understanding of the prospect company's needs and wants and, if necessary, your contact's role in the company:

"What level of innovation are you looking for?"
"Are you fully satisfied with your current direction, or are you looking to make substantial changes?"
"Ms. Smith, do you have final buying authority?"
"Ms. Smith, are you the final arbiter when it comes to strategy?"

Based on the answers to these questions, you may want to modify the next stage of your presentation. In any event, this second stage should be as brief as the nature of your offerings allow. One of the highest tributes of flattery you can deliver to a mid-level executive is a show of respect for her time. Twenty minutes is the upper limit for the whole presentation, and fifteen is even better. This said, the second part of your presentation, focusing on your offerings, should be the briefest part of the presentation. Hit the highlights only, which means that you should emphasize the benefits. As for specifics, refer the executive(s) to brochures, handouts, and/or a website. Of course, if you are specifically asked for detailed information, be prepared to provide it—and provide it enthusiastically.

The second part of the presentation should emphasize the following benefits for *mainstreamers*:

We are team players.
We make you look good.
We are all about competence, not showboating.
We bring stability, security, and reliability.
We help you stay on course.
What we provide is widely accepted throughout the industry.

For *decision makers*, the benefits must be more aggressive:

Innovation.
Being ahead of the curve.
Not just responsive to the marketplace, anticipative of it.
We provide you with control.
We operate at a sophisticated level.
We will get you noticed.

Finally, end the presentation by bringing the first two sections together. Present your case for why you and your company are the best business partners for the prospect company. Match the offerings enumerated in the second part of the presentation to the opportunities and challenges you have defined in the first part. Present your company and your products as just the right fit with the prospect, whether you are speaking to a mainstreamer or a decision maker.

And, as always, listen—listen and respond directly and thoroughly to what you hear. If your prospect offers corrections, modifications, amendments, or additional information to the material in the first part of your presentation, respond to these. If your line of widgets requires a source of reliable power, for instance, and your prospect has just told you that his company is planning to expand into India, where the power grid is notorious for its unreliability, point out that your current filter, surge suppressor, and battery-backup technology leads the industry. "It's precisely the fail-safe technology you need in unreliable power environments. Your equipment and your production will be secure."

More About Selling to the Decision Maker

When selling just below the C-level suite, the decision-maker executive is the most challenging prospect, but also the most promising. She may ask tough questions, but if you succeed in persuading her to decide in your favor, she is likely to become an advocate for you and your offerings because she sees you as a means to further her own advancement. For this reason, be certain that you approach the decision maker as a peer—a professional who is meeting with another professional. Present yourself as a prospective partner, one who wields the clout in your own firm to deliver fully on whatever you promise. Present yourself to her as a colleague capable of solving the problems of a colleague.

When you approach a decision maker, don't come out selling. Begin a discussion. If you are operating from a formal presentation, the first part of that presentation—your review of the prospect company—serves this introductory purpose. If you are selling more informally, then make certain that you begin by raising issues related to the needs and direction of the prospect company. Do this before you launch into your own offerings. Of course, if the executive indicates a desire to cut to the chase and is eager to hear about your goods and services, give her what she wants without delay. Just start selling.

Speak the language of business. While expressing an understanding and appreciation of the prospect company's vision and direction, quantify all of your offerings in dollar figures whenever possible. Put the greatest emphasis on value—that is, on return on investment (ROI). At the end of the day, the objective of any executive is to be seen as contributing to the improvement of profitability.

Be aware of time, and don't waste it. Get to your points quickly. This does not mean you should rush or start speed-talking. Instead, endeavor to deliver calmly and professionally the most meaning in the fewest possible words. If the *executive* wants to converse at greater length, by all means listen and engage. Getting to the point and saving time is your job. Anything the prospect wants to say to you should be given all the time necessary.

Don't lie. It never works, at least not for long. Besides, telling the truth provides its own emotional energy that makes a presentation come across as valuable and worth listening to.

Consider offering something for nothing. Any information or insight you can "give" to your prospect with no expectation of return will be perceived as inordinately valuable. It creates a bond, provided that the advice or analysis is offered gratis and not in unspoken expectation of a quid pro quo.

WORDS AND PHRASES TO USE WITH MAINSTREAMERS

Absolute

Agreement

Approval

Be insulated

Buy it and forget it

Certified

Consensus

Everyone accepts these results/
    will be pleased

Evolutionary change

Full integration

Fully guaranteed

Gradual change

Integral

Keep improving

Limit your exposure

No apologies will ever be required

No disruptions/interruptions/
    surprises—ever

Nothing to justify

Outcomes will be predictable

Prevailing

Protect yourself

Proved

Regular as clockwork

Rely on it/us

Safe course

Satisfaction

Seamless integration

Sensible

Steady advance

Steady as she goes

Supports your current direction

Team commitment/player

Totally turnkey

We blend in to your organization

We're right in line with you

Won't have to stick your neck out

You'll certainly have nothing to apologize for

WORDS AND PHRASES TO AVOID WITH MAINSTREAMERS

Accountability

All new

Bold

Break with the past

Can't think of everything

Defend

Don't worry about it

Explain

Get out in front

Groundbreaking

Guess

Improbable

Justify

Lead the pack

Makes a break with

New course

Not fully understood

Outrun the competition

Possible

Sharp departure

Shift direction

Stand out

Stuff happens

Take a chance

There is a risk

Unexpected

Unprecedented

Unusual

You never know

WORDS AND PHRASES TO USE WITH DECISION MAKERS

A beta revolution for you

A genuine discovery

A new experience/twist

A step ahead

A whole new dimension

Advance

Ahead of its time/the pack

Be seen as a pacesetter/trendsetter

Beta

Bold decision

Breakthrough

Creative

Cutting edge

Fresh approach/idea

Get noticed

Get you noticed

Hardly traditional

Innovate with us

Lead the beta culture

Major breakthrough

Never look back

New departure

Our best discovery

Out in front

Out of the box

Pioneering

Rare

Revolutionary change

Set the trend

Several steps ahead

Stick your neck out

Thought leadership

Truly innovative

Unique approach

Unlike any other on the market today

Unprecedented

When evolutionary change isn't enough

WORDS AND PHRASES TO AVOID WITH DECISION MAKERS

A known quantity

Accepted standard

An old favorite/standby

Approved

Business as usual

Can't go wrong with a classic

Comfortable

Dependable

Honored tradition

If it ain't broke, why fix it?

It just works

It's worked well in the past

Mainstream

No surprises

On a steady course

Proved classic

Refined

Reliable

Status quo

The usual

Time-tested

Tried and true

Updated classic

Won't rock the boat

CHAPTER 11

Sell an Entrepreneur/ Small Business Owner

Throughout this book, we have emphasized two consumer motivations that each sales professional must address and address persuasively: *needs* and *wants*. Needs are mostly about the features of a product or service: how the merchandise functions, what it's made of, what it does. Wants are mostly about the benefits of an item: how it makes or promises to make the owner or user feel. By way of illustration, consider that an overnight shipping service fills a need for overnight delivery. Overnight delivery is also the main *feature* of the "product" this business markets. The *benefit* of the product is that overnight delivery makes the user feel powerful, effective, and confident. Getting an important shipment delivered overnight, on time, and securely gives the user peace of mind. Such feelings are wants rather than needs, but they are very important and can certainly be for many consumers a most compelling reason to pay a premium for overnight shipping.

Many, probably most, products appeal to both needs and wants. Consider, for instance, the automobile. It fills a simply defined *need* for personal transportation. The *want* it addresses, however, is a far more complex set of feelings that, complex though they are, may be easily illustrated. A middle-aged, mousy little man in a beat-up minivan is still a middle-aged, mousy little man when he is behind the wheel of a brand-new BMW, but he probably doesn't feel nearly so mousy or so middle aged.

The duality of needs and wants, of utility and feeling, of features and benefits, is universal in selling, but nowhere is it more evident or more important than in selling to an entrepreneur or small business owner. For this class of prospective customer, feeling—attitude—is typically a key factor in buying decisions. Understand this: While a minority of entrepreneurs have dreams of growing their tiny start-up into a massive megacorporation—the Apple Computer that began in a garage, then grew into a world power—the vast majority of small business owners want nothing more or less than to create and run a successful enterprise that provides a sustainable living while freeing them from the necessity of putting up with bureaucracy, bosses, and the layoffs that come with leveraged buyouts. If you can tune yourself into this mind-set and value orientation, you will be perfectly positioned to create the level of rapport needed to sell the entrepreneur and small business owner.

SELL YOUR RELEVANCE

Sales professionals frequently grumble that small business owners and entrepreneurs are inherently suspicious and tend to reject their advances out of hand. Although small- and medium-size businesses outnumber big corporations in the United States by approximately 45 to 1, entrepreneurs do have a high tendency to respond to sales pitches by saying, "Your product just doesn't apply to me. My business is very, very unique—one of a kind."

Don't make the mistake of interpreting this as a brush-off line. Instead, always assume that whatever a prospect tells you is the truth—at least from her perspective. The truth is that most entrepreneurs really do *feel* unique, even if this is not *objectively* the case. The message they send is far more important than any correlation it may or may not have with objective truth. When the small business owner tells you that "your product doesn't apply to me," she is really saying "You are not making me feel special. I am unique, but you just don't get it."

To build business with an entrepreneur, begin by speaking directly to his feelings of being unique. Treat him as if he and his business really are unprecedented and one of a kind. Understand that if the entrepreneur had his druthers, he would not buy anything that was not specifically crafted for him and his business exclusively. Your task is to get as close to this custom-made ideal as you can. Impossible? Well, just think of the massive global chain of hamburger franchises that thrived for years on the promise of creating custom cuisine. Its slogan said it all: *Have it your way.*

This should be your message to the entrepreneurial prospect. *Have it your way.* It identifies a key benefit you must convey to sell *your* relevance to the *entrepreneur's* needs.

On a somewhat more "practical" level—that is, a level that partakes of the realm of benefits (feelings) as well as the realm of features (functions)—is the desire small business owners have for simple, easy-to-use, low-maintenance, flat-learning-curve products. Consider that most of these customers are some variation on a one-man band. They don't have a lot of employees or a lot of time, and they are very anxious to minimize the demands on energy and attention that are already stretched thin. For this reason, put the emphasis on how your product or service will cut through complexity to simplify the entrepreneur's life and reduce demands on her personal time, yet without unduly taxing the company's resources.

In their struggle to achieve independence from bosses and bureaucracies, entrepreneurs often end up becoming slaves of time. They find that there are too few hours in each day to get everything done. Eager to reclaim the independence that drove them out of the corporate environment in the first place, they crave products and services that simplify rather than add to the complexity of their lives. The less that gets between them and hands-on, expedited control of their business activities, the better. It is not that they want to move fast, but that they want to be able to take rapid action when action is required. The objective, always, is to *get it done.*

Position Your Product or Service

Make it clear that you offer practical simplicity that is customized to the customer's specifications. Preface your pitch by providing assurance:

"Mary, before we get into the specifics of our product line, let me highlight the two leading qualities of what we offer. First, everything we sell is designed to be practical—to simplify your life, to let you get your job done faster. Second, everything we offer is highly customizable to your unique needs, and we will help you create precisely the solutions that work best for you and for you exclusively."

Position Your Firm

Despite their displays of independence and maverick spirit, entrepreneurs usually feel like underdogs, even victims, especially when it comes to dealing with vendors. They assume that most suppliers naturally favor their biggest customers, their corporate customers, who, of course, represent more business for them. For this reason, small business owners may be suspicious that you are not going to offer them the best deal, let alone anything approaching most-favored-customer status.

Depending on the nature of your product or service, it may well be that higher-volume customers will get lower unit prices. If this is the case, don't misrepresent the facts to your prospect. Do make it clear, however, that you *are* giving him the best unit price available in consideration of the modest amount of his purchase. Most customers understand and accept volume pricing. What they cannot accept is being treated unfairly.

This said, the entrepreneur's greatest concern is probably not price so much as wanting the assurance that his needs will be accommodated and that he will not be ignored or passed over when you and your firm have bigger customers to deal with.

Proactively counter these anxieties by presenting your firm as a team of people, not a monolithic corporation. Emphasize your ethic of responsiveness to customer needs. Make it clear that your team will mesh with *the customer's* schedule. Present yourself as *the customer's* advocate within *your* organization. You see yourself as a partner in your customer's success.

Again, tell the truth. When you present your organization as flexible, responsive, and willing to make accommodations to the entrepreneur's unique requirements (or what she *perceives* as her unique requirements), be certain that your firm really is prepared to do what you promise it will do. Do be aware, however, that you probably will rarely be called on to actually make special accommodations. What's most important to creating a rapport conducive to a sustained and productive business relationship with the entrepreneur is that you give her the feeling that she can rely on you to accommodate her—should that need ever arise.

One word of caution about presenting your company's flexibility. Avoid giving the impression that you are so flexible that it will be left to the customer to make every single decision. While the entrepreneur wants to be accommodated and wants to have the feeling of control, most of the time what he wants even more is for *you* and *your* "people" to deliver turnkey service that relieves him of having to attend to burdensome and time-consuming details. Your best move is to present your organization in a capsule statement like this:

"What you get when our team and yours work together is our responsiveness and flexibility. We can accommodate your unique needs. We also understand that the last thing you want is more details to sort out. So we offer turnkey solutions that are both thorough and fully accountable. Let us do all the follow through, so you don't ever have to."

WORDS AND PHRASES TO USE

Be in charge/independent	Unique
Call the shots/your own shots	We adapt to you
	We are flexible
Choice is yours	We follow through so you don't have to
Customize	
Direct	We have the flexibility
Freedom	We will accommodate you
Instant	We'll take care of the details
Mesh	You are unique
Partner	You have unique needs
Perfect fit	You need total control over your business
Simple	
Success	You set the schedule
Take charge/command	You're in charge/the boss

WORDS AND PHRASES TO AVOID

Absolute	Pro-forma
Company policy	Rigid about it
Employee	Same for everyone
Growth	Sophisticated
Highly structured	Standard
No choice	Supervise
Obligatory	The way it's always done
One size fits all	Theoretical understanding
Organization	Uniform
Policy	Universal

SELL CONTROL AND INDEPENDENCE

Regardless of what the entrepreneurial prospect does or what she sells, the probability is that her choice to pursue a small business career is a choice born of attitude and lifestyle. The small business owner values:

Calling the shots.
Being independent as well as in charge.
Doing things *his* way.
Having total control and having the feeling of total control.

As the physician's celebrated Hippocratic Oath begins with a pledge to "First, do no harm," so you should approach the entrepreneur in this spirit.

- Avoid any suggestion that you or your firm intend to exert any form of authority over her. This means shunning any mention of phrases such as "our company policy" or "our regulations" or "our terms" or "our requirements."
- Don't call a contract a *contract*. Use the term *agreement* instead.
- To the degree possible, present yourself and your firm as providers, facilitators, and partners, not as vendors and creditors.

- Never put the entrepreneur in a position in which he thinks of himself as reporting to you or answering to you.
- In the course of the sales presentation, do not ask questions that require or seem to require the prospect to report quarterly or yearly results, to explain (in the sense of justify) a course of action, or to justify a particular decision.
- If you need to make a further appointment, give the prospect the choice of time and place. Never put her in the position of answering what appears to be your summons.
- Even as you provide turnkey services intended to make the small business owner's life easier, take care to avoid making him believe he is being compelled to accept your decisions or your authority.

Although you do want to sell value—and make no mistake, saving money and getting value for money are critically important to the small business owner—keep in mind that the typical entrepreneur is motivated even more strongly by a desire for freedom. Counterintuitive though it may seem, this means that you should actually avoid such corporate-sounding terms as *growth* and *profitability*.

Suggest *growth* as an objective to an entrepreneur, and you are likely to stir fears of sacrificing freedom by relinquishing control. Most entrepreneurs are more interested in "right-sizing" rather than in growing, and for them, the "right size" means just big enough to make money but comfortably small enough for them to maintain hands-on control.

As for *profitability*, the word smacks of bureaucracy, reporting requirements, and obligations to others. It is more or less an abstraction rather than a concrete reality. *Cash flow* and *cash on hand* mean far more to the small business owner than *profitability*.

It is not just that terms like *growth* and *profitability* are not top-of-mind priorities for the small business owner, but that they actually provoke anger, resentment, and anxiety. Don't impose corporate values on a resolutely anti-corporate customer. Instead, let him know you are on his page and in his corner:

"You are clearly someone who wants to maintain your ability to call your own shots. Independence is a top priority for you. I understand that. I appreciate it. I admire it. It's one reason my team and I enjoy working with entrepreneurs. Each is unique, but just about all of them are fiercely independent. We would love to partner with you in your independence."

SELL A COMPETITIVE EDGE

Giving the entrepreneurial prospect the *right* feelings is crucial not only to making the sale, but to positioning yourself and your company for an ongoing relationship with the small business owner. This said, feelings are not enough to create a business bond for the long haul. Take the next step, which is to connect your support of the entrepreneurial attitude—the embrace of freedom and control—with success in business. Show how your offerings will help give the prospect a competitive edge or, better yet, will sharpen the competitive edge she already has or believes she has.

EXAMPLE

"You and your customers already know the value of being a small, scrappy, super-agile competitor. You can move in fast and do things the corporate guys simply cannot. Your customers appreciate the individualized service you give them—your responsiveness to them. They enjoy dealing with people rather than policies. By serving your <product or service> needs in a direct, flexible, responsive, and absolutely reliable way, we want to maximize your ability to give your customers that extra-mile service. We want to give you everything you need to keep your competitive edge razor-sharp. The more freedom you have, the more you can do for your customers—give them value your bigger competitors just cannot deliver."

WORDS AND PHRASES TO USE

Achieve peak performance	Deliver the best
Always keep advancing	Everything you need to succeed
Brilliant products	For top performance every time
Count on us	High-performance tools

Improve/keep your edge

Maintain peak performance/
    your edge

Maximum effort

Optimum accuracy

Performance—every time!

Promise much, deliver more

Proved performers

The best materials

The ultimate in performance

We define performance

We help you to define
    performance

We will help you consistently
    exceed expectations

When performance counts

Yes, you can!

WORDS AND PHRASES TO AVOID

Can it wait?

Don't get shut out

Only so much we can do about it

Relax

Take it easy

We need lead time

We'll do our best

You're on the list

You're the next in line

SELL VALUE

After selling benefits customized to the entrepreneurial mind-set and cultural orientation, and after adding to this your assurance that you will make an important contribution to the prospect's competitive edge, it is finally time for you to address issues of price—which, as in virtually all selling scenarios, is a topic that should be framed less in terms of *cost* than of *value*. In the case of the small business owner, however, it is even more helpful for you to define *value* quite directly as a *true bargain*. For whatever ideals of freedom and control an entrepreneur may sincerely have, in the end, his financial resources constrain and dictate much of what he can and cannot do.

    Bear in mind the following:

1. Entrepreneurs and small business owners think of the company's cash as *their* cash.
2. When they spend company funds, entrepreneurs and small business owners feel that they are digging into their own pockets.

3. Entrepreneurs and small business owners tend to think of cost versus value on virtually a dollar-for-dollar basis. The question they continually ask themselves is "I'm expected to spend $XXX. Am I really getting $XXX worth of value for my money?"

For these three reasons, avoid presenting your prospect with nothing but prices—flat figures in isolation from anything else. Instead, always provide a context that frames your price as a high value—or, more to the point, a true bargain.

EXAMPLE

"Just so I'm sure I am adequately communicating the true value this purchase represents, let me tell you that it will cost you no more than the equivalent of what you receive for billing one of your clients X hours. For this investment, you will purchase not only a great <product> customized to your unique requirements, but also a full year of personalized support from our tech team. You'll be up and running from day one, and we'll commit to keep you up and running every day after that."

WORDS AND PHRASES TO USE

A true bargain	Keep more money in your pocket
Bang for your buck	Lets you manage costs
Consistent/great/high value	Low cost of operation
Help control costs	Maximum/significant value
Increased efficiency	The cost is comparable to . . .
Investment	What is your time worth?
Keep control of your costs	Will pay for itself

WORDS AND PHRASES TO AVOID

Cheap	No one said it would be cheap
Cut-rate	Sometimes you just have to throw money at a problem
Expensive but worth it	
I can't work with that budget	Spend
I wish I could give you a better deal	That's what it costs
I'm sorry about the price	

CHAPTER 12

Sell a Professional

"Professionals" is a broad category that can be difficult to define. For the purpose of thinking about effective sales communication, however, we can zero in on two categories: medical professionals and attorneys. It is also the case that these days, many professionals are no longer solo operators but work in organizations, such as hospitals and large legal firms, which typically have dedicated administrators, office managers, purchasing departments, and purchasing managers. When selling in these corporate-size situations, you still need to prepare yourself with knowledge of the professional's field, but you should also consult Chapter 9, which specifically addresses selling to purchasing managers in a corporate environment. In this chapter, we will focus exclusively on sales calls made directly to medical office managers, physicians, and attorneys.

RULE NUMBER ONE: PROS ARE PEOPLE

Most of us hold professionals in special esteem—and quite rightly, too. They are, after all, individuals of achievement and distinction, with years of education, training, and experience behind them. Lives and fortunes depend on them. Businesses and families rely on them. They have accepted heavy responsibilities, which they discharge on a daily basis. They do deserve our respect.

This said, they don't merit our awe.

In the end, pros are people, too. The key secret of selling business-to-business is to learn and always bear in mind that no business ever actually does business with another business. It is *people* within the business who do business with other people in the other business. This principle is especially important to apply to selling the professional. You need to approach the professional prospect as a person, a person with whom you want to do business.

Most of us have picked up from the cultural environment a prejudice against mixing sales with "the professions." Make the necessary effort to overcome this prejudice. If you simply assume that in order to sell to a doctor or a lawyer you need to stop selling and simply communicate "the facts"—that is, the *features*—of your product or service on a high and "pure" intellectual level, you almost certainly will have a great deal of trouble selling. Merely parading your merchandise in front of *any* prospect and then leaving her to her own devices, telling her, in effect, to draw her own conclusions, is not effective selling. At best, it's rolling the dice.

So, the big "difference" when it comes to selling to a professional is that there really isn't a *basic* difference between selling to a doctor or a lawyer and selling to any other prospect in business. It may require you to make a conscious exercise of will and imagination, but do look beyond the white coat and the law books on the shelves. Look instead directly at the person—the human prospect—who is looking back at you. Sell to that person. Work at understanding his wants as well as his needs. The needs are pretty easy to grasp. The customer who is a professional requires products or services with certain specific features to satisfy his professional obligations. You know that, and he knows that. What neither of you may know, however, is that the professional is most likely to actually *buy* those offerings that also provide the benefits that promise to give him not just what he needs, but also what he wants.

Sell to Your Customer, Not Your Customer's Client

If you assume that most professionals are dedicated to their patients or clients, you are making what is, for the most part, a reasonably accurate assumption. Despite its accuracy, however, it is *not* a particularly useful assumption on which to build a sales presentation. Many salespeople focus their appeal to professionals by selling the benefits of their offerings to patients and clients. This sounds reasonable, and in fact, it is important. Yet it is far more urgent to hold uppermost in your mind that *your* prospect is the doctor or the lawyer who is in front of you. It is not *his* patient or *her* client—people you will never even meet. When even the most dedicated doctor or lawyer is in the position of being a consumer, he or she has just one pressing question uppermost in mind: *What's in it for* me? Or: *What's* my *benefit?*

Without doubt, a physician wants to cure her patients. She also wants—for herself—to experience less complexity, less anxiety, less frustration, and a lot more peace of mind in the process of achieving the cure. Much the same is true for lawyers. They want to do well for their clients, but they are harried and pressured and distracted at every turn. They crave simplicity, clarity, confidence, and yes, peace of mind. But they rarely get these and certainly not with any degree of permanence.

Simplicity, clarity, confidence, and peace of mind—these are the benefits you should be selling first and foremost to professionals. With a few deft words, you should be painting for them pictures of a better, happier, easier life. Your painting complete, your next move is to put them into the picture.

Professionals—especially physicians, dentists, and others in the medical field—are bombarded by a vast array of products in specialty fields that change and evolve very quickly. The result is a welter of time-consuming complexity—a kind of intellectual fog. Always remember that the best salesperson is the person the prospect sees as a solver of problems. The fog of complexity is a terrible problem. Solve it the moment you enter the professional's space. Find ways to cut through the complexity in order to trigger a sale.

In his blog (http://mavermanagement.blogspot.com/2008/07/marketing-and-selling-to-professionals.html), John Maver, president of Maver Management Group, cites an example of persuading dentists to use or recommend a specific pharmaceutical product to treat "mild to moderate gingivitis."

The *trigger* his salespeople presented to dentists was a simple, common symptom. The dentists were told that if a patient noticed bleeding gums when he brushed or flossed, they should diagnosis "mild to moderate gingivitis." They were further persuaded that the treatment of choice for that diagnosis was the product Maver was in charge of marketing.

The lesson here is this. Simplify. Reduce the complexity that surrounds and confounds all professionals by defining unambiguous, straightforward problems or needs for which *you* have the appropriate—indeed, the perfect—solution. While this approach certainly addresses the needs of the patient or client—Look, Ma! No more gingivitis!—it also very directly provides a key benefit to *your* customer, the professional, whose working day—whose very life—has been made that much simpler, better, and more enjoyable, all thanks to you and your merchandise.

SELL A MEDICAL PROFESSIONAL

Your object at the outset must be to identify and address the compelling benefits your prospect seeks. Begin by appreciating the different roles of the medical professionals you may approach.

In many practices, your contact will not be a physician, but an office manager. You can count on her feeling that everyone—the physician as well as his patients—depends on her. The benefits she is looking for include:

- Maintaining the big picture in the practice.
- Staying in control of everything every day.
- Making certain that everyone involved in the practice gets what he or she needs when he or she needs it.

When your customer is the physician, you should get to understand as much as you can about the nature of his practice. Is the doctor in a field dominated by cutting-edge advanced research? Or is the doctor in a field such as family practice or primary care, where most of the problems encountered are of an everyday nature and the focus is on providing initial diagnosis, reliable direction, and a caring presence?

In approaching the research-driven physician, understand that his drive is to stay on the cutting edge. He values products and services that will help him to:

- Make discoveries.
- Apply discoveries.
- Keep informed of new developments.
- Make a major impact on the life and welfare of his patients.
- Break through and think outside of the box.
- Be a leader.

In selling to the primary care physician, you should assume that she seeks anything that will facilitate her daily practice and her close relationship with her patients. Most likely, she wants to:

- Be independent and maintain her independence.
- Minimize or cut through bureaucracy.
- Have hands-on contact with patients, not get buried in paperwork.
- Feel fulfilled in the daily practice of good medicine.

EXAMPLES

An approach to the medical office manager:

"I see how busy this practice is, and I thank you for giving me the opportunity to present some software products that will help you to stay on top of everything that goes on here—no matter *what* goes on. It must be quite a feeling to know that everyone depends on you, all the doctors as well as their patients. I'm sure that you would like to be fully assured and fully confident that everyone will get what they need at all times.

"Our new tracking and scheduling software products are custom-designed for medical managers who are at the very hub of activity—professionals who need innovative but commonsense tools that simplify their lives rather than add yet another level of complexity. Our programs are designed by people who have walked a mile in your shoes, people who understand just what it is like to be under pressure. The solutions they have created in this product are based on many, many conversations with managers just like you. The result, we are confident, is the best tool of its kind ever created, and we believe that managers like you have earned the best tools in the field, tools that will make your professional life not only easier but more rewarding and that will give you the peace of mind that comes with knowing you are serving everyone who depends on you."

WORDS AND PHRASES TO USE

360-degree view

Accurate assessment/information/
   report

Anticipate

Call on us

Clarify

Commanding view

Control

Coordinate

Cut through

Data

Direct relationship/route

Easy

Everything revolves around you

Full information/report

Here for you

High-ground view

Hub

Information

Instant action/response

Make clear

Manage

One-stop shop

Proactive

Puts you at the center

Quick

Rely on us

Respond/responsive

Save time

Simple/simplify

Stay ahead/on top of

Total control

Your go-to source

WORDS AND PHRASES TO AVOID

All alone

Analyze

Be independent

Get back to you on that

Go your own way

Highly technical

I don't have that information

Not easy/sure

Put it on hold

Requires some thought

Stand alone

Very complicated

Approach to the research-driven physician:

"You are a leader in your field. You have to be. Our custom-targeted re-search abstract series gives you what you need to continue making the breakthroughs that provide the best hope and best care to your patients. We understand that you not only need to stay out in front, you need to feel the confidence and assurance that you have ongoing, uninterrupted access to the most important emerging developments in your field. You also want to be confident that you are seeing these developments in the context of all the best science.

"We bring to you our combined experience as data engineers, medical professionals, and medical journalists. We put this experience at your complete disposal with exclusive and exclusively customized scholarly and clinical abstract services that ensure you will never be left behind."

WORDS AND PHRASES TO USE

Accepted protocols	Evolving
Acumen	Fighting the battle
Advanced	Finding answers
Always exploring/out in front	Forward-looking
Balanced	Going farther
Beyond question	Informed risk taking
Bold strides	Inquiring
Breaking through	Intensely curious
Breakthrough	Learning
Certainty	Making a difference/a real impact/
Continually updated	strides
Curious	Progress/progressive
Current	Reliable data
Data	Taking the lead
Discovery	The right diagnosis

WORDS AND PHRASES TO AVOID

Approved	Avoiding risk
Assume	Conjecture

Flexible standards	No pressure
Guesswork	Playing it safe
Intuitive	State-of-the-art
Middle of the road	Teamwork

SELL AN ATTORNEY

Like medical professionals, attorneys are first and foremost human beings, and a human salesperson must appeal to them on a human level. Nevertheless, we cannot overlook three factors that frequently set attorneys apart from other prospects.

1. They are trained to trust no one. This is a hurdle going into any sale to a lawyer.
2. Even in this era of attorneys advertising on TV and elsewhere, most lawyers are wary of overtly selling or appearing to overtly sell their professional services. This means they also tend to be resistant to those who try to sell *to* them. Another built-in hurdle.
3. Lawyers take the confidential attorney-client relationship very, very seriously. They accordingly have a kneejerk fear of any third-party consultant or vendor whom they perceive as a possible threat to the intimacy of that hallowed (and legally sanctioned) relationship.

The first two hurdles can be cleared by means of a single strategy. It is to accept and to embrace both the lawyer's aversion to selling and her inherent inclination to distrust you. Just resign yourself to the fact that these both come with the territory. Confront and overcome these hurdles by taking steps to build trust. Your ultimate objective is to transform the lawyer-prospect's perception of you from *salesperson* to *member of the team*.

The process of this transformation is a kind of wooing, and as with any effective wooing, it is best to start it slowly. Be prepared to be patient. Break the ice by asking the lawyer about issues of interest and concern *to him*. If you've done a good job of researching before making the sales call, use some of that information now.

Let's say your prospect has a significant practice in real estate law. You might begin the discussion by asking how the slowly improving housing market is affecting his practice these days. Such a discussion is especially helpful if your service or product relates in some special way to real estate law, but whether it does or does not, your purpose at this point is less to sell than it is to show that you are engaged with the lawyer's practice. You are building a relationship. You are replacing distrust with something at least approaching trust. The more you can get the prospect to talk, the better—not only because you will learn something, but because by talking to you your prospect invests in you, and you thereby acquire value as well as trustworthiness in his eyes.

Discreetly share useful information. Draw on your experience with your other customers in the legal profession. Always take care, however, to avoid revealing any confidences. Your objective is merely to establish your highly valued presence in *this lawyer's* field.

Pay attention to the nonverbal aspects of presence as well as to the content of your verbal messages. Lawyers dress well—usually conservatively, but stylishly and well. You should dress like a lawyer when you call on a lawyer.

Lawyers also take comfort in order and structure. For this reason, give serious thought to emailing an outline-formatted agenda in advance of your sales call. Invite your prospect to comment. Invite her to make additions.

In the course of your meeting, when you have reached the point at which you have a sense that you have built at least some level of rapport and trust, begin the sales process proper: the actual presentation of your product or service. When you do this, you are very likely to encounter resistance based on the prospect's fear of being manipulated or, despite whatever rapport has been established, even deceived. Your objective is to put the prospect in the position of perceiving that this fear is substantially outweighed by the much more urgent danger of failing to secure a service or a product her competitors are about to possess or already possess. The benefit you are selling is the feeling of being ahead of the competition. It is a feeling of confidence and peace of mind. Promote this benefit, and the attorney's natural fear of being conned and duped by a salesperson will recede in comparison to her more acute fear of lacking something in her competition's arsenal.

EXAMPLE

"The one thing you *never* want is to go into a trial feeling yourself at a disadvantage. Your competitors are using jury consultants. You know that. What you may not know is that they are diving so deeply into that sector that they are investing disproportionately in it. You definitely do not need the feeling that to match your adversaries and competitors, you have to follow their lead by letting the tail wag the dog. What we can give you is jury-consulting expertise that is just as much as you need to gain the edge without having to go over the edge. It's all about leveraging a *little* control to get *all* the control you need.

"Our hybrid artificial intelligence–human intelligence approach saves you time, resources, and cash, while delivering all the sophistication you need. We never make you feel that we have intruded and hijacked your case. As far as your client is concerned, our presence will be totally transparent.

"Our software and our service have been created by and are backed by a unique team of software engineers and attorneys. Working together, they have bridged the chasm between technology and the demands of your legal practice, so that you don't have to worry about it. Ever. The result, for you, is bulletproof performance that has impact far beyond your investment in money and time."

WORDS AND PHRASES TO USE

A strategy in the truest sense	Gain control
Adaptable	Gives you the competitive edge/
Anticipates the future	the insight you need
As close to automatic as you	Inoculates you against risk
can get	Irresistible
Bulletproof	Leverage the outcome
Continue to win	Like clockwork
Credible	Maintain control
Dominate your adversary/your	Minimize stress/exposure
competition	No surprises

Nothing hidden
Overwhelmingly persuasive
Readily implemented
Reduces your dependence on
   others

Shapes influence
Sophisticated approach
Tested approach

WORDS AND PHRASES TO AVOID

As practical as possible
Close enough
Common sense
Flexible interpretation
Highly technical
High-tech
Industry standard
It is a bold move
More or less

Pro forma
Reasonably predictable
Take a chance
Temporary fix
The value isn't immediately
   apparent
Trust me
Why not?
You have to have *some* trust

PART THREE

SPEAK THE LANGUAGE OF COMPLETE SATISFACTION

These days, forward-looking businesses strive to integrate or at least coordinate the sales and service functions. In the end, all business is about serving the customer. The six chapters of Part Three focus on traditional customer service while also closely relating customer service to sales. The objective is to achieve complete customer satisfaction, which means doing more than making *a* sale or fixing *a* problem. The objective is to create one loyal customer after another.

CHAPTER 13

Master the Service Vocabulary

Creating customer satisfaction depends on factors ranging from the quality of your product or service, to your competition, to the conditions in your particular marketplace. It also depends on an intangible quality, which is how your customers feel about you and your organization. It depends, to a significant degree, on the rapport that exists between company and customer.

Rapport can be difficult enough to create in face-to-face situations, but at least in a live encounter you have such rapport builders to call on as a warm handshake and a smile. On the telephone, however, all you have is your voice and your words.

CREATE A CLIMATE FOR SATISFACTION

In itself, rapport does not create customer satisfaction, but it creates a climate that makes customer satisfaction possible. On the phone, your voice—even more than your words—is the most important ingredient in creating positive rapport. If you are fortunate enough to possess a pleasing phone voice, congratulations; however, even if that voice does not come naturally to you, you can work at cultivating a rhythm and tone that are a pleasure to hear. It is not all that difficult. Begin by focusing on the following:

1. *The pace of your speech.* Most of us speak too fast. So just try slowing down. Really concentrate on speaking a little more slowly than you are normally inclined to do. Your pace on the phone should be slower than your customary conversational pace.

2. *The pitch of your voice.* Unless you already have a deep voice, consider consciously trying to lower the pitch of your telephone voice. Most people perceive lower-pitched as more authoritative as well as more pleasing than higher-pitched voices. Surprisingly, this rule of thumb applies to women and to men equally.

    As a rule, side effects are unpleasant things, but in the case of lowering the pitch of your voice, you get the bonus of a very positive side effect. The exercise will force you to speak more slowly and distinctly even as it lowers your register.

3. *Stand when you speak on the phone.* Standing not only brings your voice down, it gives it more power and more authority.

4. *Enunciate.* Impart full value to each word, and ensure that you are understood. This not only saves time and prevents errors, it tends to create satisfaction in your customer rather than the irritation that arises if he has to expend effort to decipher slurred, mumbled, or garbled speech. In addition, careful enunciation tells your listener that you are an intelligent human being. The person on the other end of the line will therefore get the feeling that you are capable of providing the service or help that she wants. For this reason, she will typically show you the level of courtesy and respect that makes doing business a pleasure.

Greetings!

Creating rapport on the phone begins with your greeting. It actually starts even before the customer has uttered a single word. Why? Because you already know what the caller wants. The caller wants *useful information.*

For this reason, load useful information into your greeting.

Instead of a simple "Hello," try the following: "Good afternoon. This is ABC Widgets, Mary Williams speaking. How may I help you?"

Three or four seconds have elapsed, and you have supplied four key pieces of information. The caller knows:

1. That she is speaking to someone who is pleasant, polite, and civil.
2. That she has contacted the place she intended to contact. By supplying this information, you have saved the caller the effort of asking if she has reached her intended objective. From the start, you have saved the customer trouble, and you have therefore solved a problem.
3. That she has reached a specific person inside the company: you, Mary Williams, genuine Homo sapiens, with a name.
4. That you are eager to help, which suggests that you are also willing to accept responsibility.

Always use the phrase *How may I help you?* in your greeting. This question, with the operative word *how*, not only conveys a helping attitude, it immediately focuses the conversation right from the start, thereby saving time and reducing the potential for frustration. Compare the simpler "May I help you?" While this is also a polite choice of words, it invites a one-word, pro forma answer: *yes.* Indeed, it's the only answer possible, since *no* would mean the caller has no reason to have called. It is, therefore, a waste of time because it provides no information of any value. In contrast, "How may I help you?" prompts the caller to explain the reason for her call.

Your objective in answering a customer service call is to convey a commitment to customer satisfaction. This means assuring your caller that you intend to take *ownership* of the call. Put yourself in the caller's place. Chances are, she harbors some anxiety that she will end up wasting valuable time and energy in a frustrating game of telephone tag, getting transferred from one person—or recorded message—to another. It is as if the customer has called in the very expectation of encountering not help but frustration and failure.

Surprise her by taking immediate ownership of her call. This means, having answered the phone, the call is *yours*. Take responsibility for it. Own it until you have answered the caller's question or solved her problem—or until you have "sold" your property, the call, to someone else who *can* answer the question or resolve the issue.

After the initial greeting and after listening to the response to "How may I help you?" give assurance: "I can take care of that for you."

Request (Never Demand) Information

After your greeting, you'll need to get the caller to give you the information you need so that you can provide the appropriate service. Take care to avoid wrecking rapport with such abrupt commands as "What's your telephone number?" "What is your account number?" or "I need your account number." Instead, ease into your *request* for information:

> YOU: . . . How may I help you?
> CALLER: I can't get my Double Y software to output to my printer.
> YOU: I can certainly help you with that.

After providing this assurance that you will provide successful aid, make your request:

> YOU: May I have the serial number of your software? Just click on "Help," then "About." You'll find the number there. With that, I can pull up the information I need to get you up and running right away.

Note that the request is phrased *as a request*, not a demand. It is also followed by an explanation of how supplying the requested information will benefit the caller—not you, not your company, not your company's protocols and policies, but the caller.

READ THE CUSTOMER'S MIND
(IN OTHER WORDS, *LISTEN*)

The single most important skill required for delivering effective customer service is effective listening, the capacity for really *hearing* what your customer is saying. It works like this:

1. Give your caller your undivided attention. Even though you are on the phone and can't be seen, resist the urge to multitask "behind the caller's back."
2. Take notes, if you need to. Be sure to tell the caller that you are taking notes: "I'm taking some notes as we speak." This lets him know that you regard his call as highly important. It is an effective way to build rapport—and, if necessary, to defuse an angry caller. Quickly jot down the main points of what the caller says.
3. Practice reflective listening. That is, reflect back to the caller the main points of what he tells you. For example:

CALLER: The motor dies when I try to do X, Y, or Z.
YOU: So it quits when you attempt X, Y, or Z. How about when you do A, B, or C? Does it function properly?
CALLER: It does.

Your caller should now feel confident that progress toward solving his problem is being made—because it is. Reinforce this progress with your response:

YOU: Good! Now I understand the extent of the problem. We're getting somewhere! The problem is located in X, Y, and Z. Here is our next step . . .

Discipline yourself to listen without intrusive interruption and, above all, without reacting in any way that suggests exasperation or loss of patience. When the caller fails to make himself clear or fails to comprehend what you are telling him, you may naturally feel like replying with a sentence that begins: "What I'm *trying* to tell you" or "Look, *this* is what I'm *trying* to tell you." These expressions are rapport killers because they communicate a harsh verdict on the caller's intelligence—or insufficiency thereof. It will do you, your company, and your customer no good to communicate such a negative message. Instead of letting such expressions of exasperation slip out, preface your umpteenth repetition with, "Let me see if I can express myself more effectively" or "Let me try to explain this better." In delivering excellent customer service, the most effective tactic is always to take the burden off the customer and put it on yourself.

WORDS OF ACKNOWLEDGMENT

The most important words in the customer service vocabulary are those that assure the customer that her concerns are valid and important—both to her and to you. These words constitute the vocabulary of acknowledgment.

WORDS AND PHRASES TO USE

A pleasure to help	Gratifying
Accept	Help/helpful
Accommodate	In your place/shoes
Action	No problem!
Agree	Patience
Apologize	Quickly
Appreciate	Recognize
Approve	Resolve quickly
Assist	Responsive
Concern/concerned	Sorry that you are not satisfied
Expedite	Support
Extra mile	Thank you
Focus	Understand how you feel/the
Grant	issue/the problem
Grateful for your patience/	Walk you through
understanding	We care

Welcome
Will assist you

Work together
You will be satisfied

WORDS AND PHRASES TO AVOID

Can't do much
Complain
Complaint
Disagree
Don't understand
Don't worry about it
Give it a shot
Has never happened before
I don't believe you

Nobody has ever complained
That just can't be
Vague
What is your complaint/problem?
What's wrong now?
Will do what I can
You must be doing something
    wrong
You're not being clear

WORDS OF CALM

Delivering effective customer service requires separating personality from issues. Whereas faulty merchandise or an error in performing a service can be fixed, people cannot be. For this reason, a vocabulary that introduces calm—that simultaneously establishes your calm competence while defusing the customer's anxiety, irritation, and (in some cases) anger—is essential to creating a climate in which product and service issues can be addressed and resolved without interference from extraneous issues related to perceived attitude, personality, and motives.

WORDS AND PHRASES TO USE

Be assured, we'll resolve this
Complete support
Explain this to me like I'm a
    two-year-old
Focus
Full support
Guarantee

I don't want you stressing
    about this
I won't hang up until you are
    completely satisfied
I'm following you perfectly
I'm listening
Leave it to me/us

Let's do this together
Let's focus on your issues with the product
Let's go over it together
Let's go through it step by step
Let's nail this down
Modify
One step at a time
Promise
Rain or shine
Resolve
Satisfy
Take all the time you need
Tell me the problem
Walk me through
Warranty
We will make it right
Work together
You are making perfect sense
You have my word
You should not have to worry
You will be satisfied

WORDS AND PHRASES TO AVOID

Against our policy
Calm down
Chill out
Don't know
Don't raise your voice
Don't talk to me like that
I can't help you with that
I'm hanging up
It is a problem for you
It's going to cost you
May take a long time
Not my area/problem
Not the way it's done
Nothing I can do about that
Slow down!
Take it easy
We're getting nowhere
You are mistaken
You don't understand
You have a problem
You have to call back

WORDS OF APOLOGY AND SOLUTION

A sincere apology goes a long way toward establishing—or reestablishing—rapport and establishing—or reestablishing—confidence and trust in a product, service, or firm. As valuable as this is, the apology is made far more powerful when it is immediately followed by the promise of a solution, resolution, or repair.

WORDS AND PHRASES TO USE

Able

Accommodate

Agree

Alternative

Apologize for the inconvenience/
personally

Appreciate your understanding

As promised

Assure

At your option

Benefit

Best case/worst case

Bottom line

Choice

Choose

Confident

Configuration

Confirmation

Do everything possible

Do you happen to have your
order number handy?

Double-check

Expedite shipment

Experience

Explain

Frustration

Grateful for your understanding

How may I help you?

I estimate

I fully understand

I want to thank you

I'm sorry to hear

If you like

Is that agreeable?

Is there anything else I can help
you with today?

It will take

It's your call

Leave the choice to you

Let's work together

My error/mistake

Necessary steps

On behalf of

Optimum

Option

Our error/mistake

Performance

Promptly

Refund

Reimburse

Replace/replacement

Resolve the problem

Respond/responsive

Satisfy

Serious

Sorry you had a problem

Support

Take comments like yours very
seriously

Thanks for your order

Together

Understanding

Up and running

We will make every effort

We'll proceed accordingly

Whatever is necessary

Which would you prefer?

Within my power

You can be certain

Your answers will help me
  determine

Your complete satisfaction is our
  top priority/our primary
  concern

WORDS AND PHRASES TO AVOID

Happens to the best of us

Margin for error

Nobody's perfect

Not our fault

Not perfect, but as good as it gets

Not something we cover

Nothing like this has ever
  happened before

Outside our area of responsibility

Some things just slip by us

Stuff happens

This is a shame

We can't be held responsible

We're not liable

We're not perfect

Within the margin of error

You can't please everybody

WORDS OF HELPING

Customer service is first and last about helping. The words you use should convey your determination to be helpful and your commitment to the welfare and satisfaction of your caller.

WORDS AND PHRASES TO USE

Accommodate your request

Advice

Aid

All that you need

Assist

At your service

Attend to it

Complete service

Correct this

Do it immediately

Everything you need

Full service

I can help with that

I understand your problem and
  know what to do

I will fix it

I will help you

I'm on it

Improve

Modify

Not a problem

On an emergency basis/urgent
  basis

Provide the help you need

This will facilitate/provide relief
Top priority
Total satisfaction
Under control
Urgent
We can take care of that
We have a remedy
We will make the repair

We will replace the part
We will take care of that
We'll expedite it
We've got what you need
Whatever it takes
You won't have to wait
You've come to the right place

WORDS AND PHRASES TO AVOID

Call back in an hour
I can't answer that
I can't help you with that
I can't predict
I don't know what to tell you
I have nothing to offer you
I'm afraid you've come to the
    wrong place

I'm putting you on hold
Stopgap
There's nothing I can do
This is not something we do
We can try
We can't be held responsible
    for this
You do have a real problem

WORDS OF CREDIBILITY

Choose words that create confidence and trust. Avoid hype, and don't make promises you know you cannot keep.

WORDS AND PHRASES TO USE

Absolute
Act with confidence
An ethic of service
Assurance
Backbone
Believe
Buy with confidence
Certainty
Commitment

Competence
Complete satisfaction/trust/
    confidence
Earn your trust
Ethical
Ethics
Guarantee
Informed judgment
Integrity

Know-how

Knowledge

No excuses

Our commitment/pledge to you

Our ethos

Put your trust in us

Rely on us

We mean what we say

We won't let you down

When you absolutely need it

You have my word

Your future

You're part of the family

You're with us now

WORDS AND PHRASES TO AVOID

Best in the world

Don't believe everything you hear about us

Don't worry about it

I think it will be okay

I wouldn't worry about it

I'm pretty sure

Just relax

Nobody can give you that kind of guarantee

Nobody is as good as we are

Our competition doesn't tell the truth

Take my word for it

We're the only vendor you can trust

You can never tell

USING THE "SOFTEN" SOLUTION

Most customer service is transacted over the phone, but you may also have the opportunity to deliver excellent service face-to-face. The big advantage here is that you have the physical presence of the customer to help guide your responses and, even more important, the customer can see *you*, including your body language. Provided that you use your body language in a positive manner, this dimension of communication can do much to enhance the service experience.

In their 1994 *Complete Business Etiquette Handbook*, Barbara Pachter and Marjorie Brody provide a convenient acronym that can readily be applied to the in-person customer service situation. They call it "SOFTEN," and it stands for *Smile, Open up, Forward lean, Tone it down, Eye contact now, and Nod*. Let's apply the SOFTEN solution to the in-person customer service situation:

■ **Smile.** The smile is universal and universally welcoming. It is the single strongest signal you can send to the world that you are open for business and open for conversation. The smile is the first facial expression infants learn, and it is probably the first expression they learn to respond to. From very early in our lives, we look for smiling faces. Unfortunately, as we grow into adulthood, smiling often comes to us less naturally. We may even have to work at generating a smile. But it is worth the effort, especially when you deliver customer service. Very often, the customer comes to you stressed and unhappy. Your smile suggests that you will make everything right again. In addition, your customer may assume that because he is coming to you with a complaint or a problem, you will *not* be happy to see her. Your smile proves him wrong—in a delightful way.

It is hard to go wrong with a smile; however, use common sense about it. If you are delivering or receiving bad news, a grin is out of place: "Unfortunately, Mr. Smith, the motor is burned out and will have to be replaced." This is bad (because presumably costly) news. This doesn't mean you have to deliver it as if you are announcing the death of a loved one, but an expression of glee will be interpreted as something like gleeful indifference or downright taunting cruelty. Deliver the bad news—"Unfortunately, Mr. Smith, the motor is burned out and will have to be replaced"—with a neutral expression, then go ahead and brighten when you provide your solution: "But not to worry. We have the replacement in stock, and you'll find that it's not as expensive as you probably think. Also, we can turn around the repair before the end of the day." Now go ahead and smile.

■ **Open up.** Smiling should also help you adopt what body language experts call "open" body language. This means that you should face the other person, avoid folding your arms across your chest (a gesture that communicates resistance), and avoid putting your hands on your hips (a gesture that conveys defiance). Keep your hands away from your mouth and face as well, since such gestures communicate worry, skepticism, impatience, boredom, and worst of all, an intent to deceive. Nevertheless, don't be afraid to gesture with your hands. Doing so makes your message and your physical presence more emphatic and more interesting. Do try to use open gestures, however, with palms upward—a universal signal of offering and giving rather than taking or, even worse, making a threat.

- **Forward lean.** In American business and professional culture, maintaining personal space can be a significant body-language issue. Most Americans are comfortable with face-to-face distances of about three feet. In general, maintain this comfort zone—but also learn to "violate" it creatively:

  - Lean forward from time to time to make an important point.
  - Lean forward to demonstrate that you are listening especially intensely when a customer has something to say that is clearly important to her.
  - Lean forward from time to time to punctuate a personal exchange so that you underscore your interest in what the other person is saying.

  When you lean forward, do not touch the other person, and do not point or gesture with a pointing finger. This is an aggressive gesture that will provoke resistance.

- **Tone it down.** Face-to-face, speak as you speak on the phone: distinctly. Never mumble. Don't let your sentences trail off. Do not speak while looking downward or away from the other person. Be aware, however, that loud volume does not equal clarity. Make the face-to-face exchange a genuine conversation, which means, above all, establish and maintain a conversational tone and volume. Don't shout, and don't speak at a high pitch. If necessary, make the conscious effort to lower your voice both in volume and pitch.

  Experienced speakers know the value of occasionally diminishing volume. Common sense may suggest that you should raise your voice when you have an important point to make. In fact, the opposite is generally most effective, especially in face-to-face conference. If you lower the volume of your voice when you get to your main point, your listener will make a special effort to concentrate and to hear you.

- **Eye contact now.** Always make eye contact with your partner in conversation. This not only communicates your interest, it powerfully conveys your trust and your trustworthiness. Should you fail to make eye contact—if you look away or if your eyes habitually wander—you send at least two destructive messages:

- You are bored with what the other person is telling you and would rather be elsewhere.
- You are hiding something. (We often speak of shifty people as specifically "shifty-eyed.")

As with the smile, it is difficult to go very far wrong by making and maintaining eye contact. Do, however, remain sensitive to your conversation partner. Don't let eye contact turn into a zombie stare or a stare-down contest. Do nothing to intimidate the other person or make him feel uncomfortable.

■ **Nod.** Listening is by definition a mostly silent enterprise; however, it is important to signal your continued interest and comprehension. You don't have to inject frequent comments into a conversation just to prove that you're listening. A universal signal of comprehension and agreement is the nod. Send this signal. Nod and then nod some more at intervals. This is a powerful body-language signal that communicates understanding and acceptance of what is being said. Furthermore, it tells the other person that you want her to continue talking. It creates positive rapport and is likely to produce what you most need to be helpful: detailed information.

CHAPTER 14

Master the Medium

This chapter is devoted to the two most important mediums for delivering customer service: the telephone and email. The Internet, including online chat and social media, already well established as a sales medium, is also fast emerging as an important platform for customer service. We will present ideas for using chat and the social web in Chapter 18.

ON THE PHONE

These days, the Internet and social web seem to get all the glory, but when a customer really wants to reach you—really needs help—it's the telephone she reaches for, not the mouse. The telephone is your customers' lifeline to you. It is the vehicle of choice for delivering personal service in an impersonal world—unless you choose to treat it as yet another electronic pigeonhole into which you sort and hold yet another "problem."

Manage This Medium

No prospective employer would ever ask you if you "know how to use a tele-phone." But, it turns out, the question is very much worth asking.

The phone rings. What do you do? Answer it, of course. But when?

If you want to create customer satisfaction, you answer within two or three rings or twenty seconds. Most customers will hang up after four to five rings—six at most, unless the caller is very determined to make contact.

And when is a customer so determined? When he feels he has a reason important or urgent enough to invest valuable time calling you and then waiting for you, ring after ring, to answer. In other words, the customer is determined when the problem is perceived as serious. Keep him waiting through more than four of five rings, and how is he likely to feel by the time you finally do pick up that phone? Well, count on talking to an angry, anx-ious customer, who has already decided what kind of company he is deal-ing with.

This, by the way, is the best-case scenario. If the caller gives up and hangs up before you pick up, you may have lost a customer. Worse, you may have created more than an ex-customer. You may have created an ex-customer eager to tell his network of friends and business associates just what kind of company yours is.

Fortunately, there is an easy way to steer clear of either scenario. Pick up the phone within twenty seconds, preferably on the first ring. But don't let overeagerness spoil the moment of contact. Make sure you don't start speak-ing until you actually pick up the phone. If you are wearing a headset, be sure you punch in the call before you start to speak. If this seems like ridiculously elementary advice, just think about how many times you have called "Smith and Jones" only to be greeted with a truncated ". . . Jones."

So now you've picked up the phone and answered the call. That's a lot, but it isn't quite enough. Give some thought to what you bring to the telephone call you are answering. Is it your own stress, annoyance, anxiety, and fatigue? All the weighty and disheveled baggage of a hectic day?

Before you greet your next caller, give some thought to what you can do to reduce or eliminate whatever factors and influences diminish your effec-tiveness on the phone.

- Do you get enough sleep? Daytime fatigue drains your patience and your effectiveness as a communicator.
- Are you hungry? A growling stomach can make the nicest of us irritable. Try not to field your most difficult calls right before lunch.
- Are you overcaffeinated? As much as many of us crave coffee, caffeine does quite a credible job of mimicking the physiological changes of anxiety and rage. Consider easing up.
- How comfortable are you? Maybe you need to turn up the air-conditioning or open a window. A hot, stuffy room puts many of us in a fighting mood—not a good attitude for creating customer satisfaction.

May I Put You on Hold?

Another of the basics of handling the telephone medium is placing a customer on hold. This is often a necessity, but if you think this poses a threat to rapport and customer satisfaction, you're right. It does. You can, however, minimize the negatives.

1. Always ask the customer's permission before putting him on hold: "May I put you on hold?"
2. If you know the hold time will be brief, say so: "May I put you on a brief hold?"
3. If you can give an accurate estimate of the duration of the hold, give it: "May I put you on hold for about thirty seconds?" If the hold time stretches significantly beyond this, return to the caller: "I need about two more minutes of your time. Do you want to remain on hold, or should I call you back?"
4. If you can *briefly* explain the purpose of the hold, do so: "May I put you on hold for about thirty seconds while I retrieve your record?"

The customer will not withhold permission—unless she really has no time or patience. If you must put her on hold and she does refuse her permission ("No, I just don't have the time"), offer to call *her* back.

If it is routinely necessary to put your callers on hold, find alternatives to silence. Forced to wait in "dead air," the caller will became impatient or even anxious, worried that he has been forgotten or accidentally disconnected. One solution is to fill the dead air of hold time with music. While this is preferable to silence, because it reassures the caller that the connection hasn't been lost, many callers find telephone music annoying. It usually sounds tinny at best, and one person's idea of music may well be another's idea of noise. The better and far more productive alternative is to use the hold time to provide something the caller can actually use and may even value— namely, *information*. Consider filling the void with recorded information that allows the caller to learn more about your company. Useful subjects include information on how the customer can make better use of your products; on the value of preventive maintenance; on your hours of operation or the location of offices and service centers; and a list of what information the caller should have on hand to make the call more productive: "To expedite service, please have your account number ready to give your Customer Service representative." If appropriate to your situation, you may use hold time to provide answers—right *now*. Consider a system that allows you to record a list of FAQs: Frequently Asked Questions. Each item might be accompanied by a number, which the customer can press on his touch-tone pad to receive a recorded answer. For example: "What does fault code 123 mean? *Press 4.*" The customer presses 4:

> Fault code 123 indicates an interrupted cycle. Switch off your unit and unplug it. Wait thirty seconds. Plug it in again and switch it back on. Often, the fault code will disappear—along with the problem.

Another creative use of hold time is to provide messages that enhance your public image or raise your profile in the community. A busy physician's office might play something like this:

> Did you know that exercising at least three times per week, thirty minutes per session, significantly improves your health and your quality of life? Our community offers a wide array of low-cost and no-cost opportunities to get in shape or stay in shape. For example . . .

If there is one message to *avoid* during the hold time it is the reminder that "your call is very important to us." Few robotic messages are better designed to provoke resentment, anger, and distrust. After all, if *my* call were really important to *you*, *you* would be talking to *me* right now. On its face, the message comes across as a lie. Avoid it.

OWNING THE CALL

These days, "customer service" is often the first of a company's operations to be outsourced. Aside from how it may impact employment numbers, outsourcing is not necessarily a bad thing—at least as long as callers request nothing but straightforward, basic information. When the issues become more difficult and demanding, however, you may not be able to outsource the call without doing damage to customer satisfaction.

The only consistently effective approach to customer service delivered on the phone is to commit totally to the caller and the call. If *you* picked up the phone, *you* own the call. If your objective is to create satisfaction, you cannot thoughtlessly give away or otherwise abandon the call. For example:

> CALLER: I ordered six Type 1 widgets on May 5. I need to change that order to Type 2 widgets, but I still need to get delivery by May 12. Can you make this happen?

Based on past experience, you believe it can be done, but you want to make sure. You could simply pass the caller off to the Shipping Department, but that would mean making the customer wait and then compelling her to repeat her story to a new person. That person may or may not have the answer, so he might end up sending the caller to yet another individual. Welcome to "call runaround."

Fortunately for the caller, you have committed yourself to owning his call, therefore you respond:

> YOU: Let me get that answer for you. I need to check with our Shipping Department, which I can do for you right now. It should take

me about two to three minutes. May I put you on hold for that long? Or would you like me to get the information and call you back with it?

This is call ownership. It requires positive action. In this case, you:

1. Assured your customer that you *will* obtain the necessary information.
2. Informed the customer of what you need to do to get her the information.
3. Told her, as specifically as possible, how long it will take.
4. Gave the *customer* options rather than forcing anything on her.

Keep the Caller in the Loop

Another secret to mastering the telephone medium is making the effort to keep your caller in the loop. Remember, he can't see what you're doing, so when you consult a record on your computer screen, verbally *share* your computer screen with him:

YOU: I can get the information you need. I'm calling up your record on my monitor. Please spell your last name for me. Thank you. You're at 1234 East Smith Street?

CALLER: Yes.

YOU: Great! Now, I see three orders, placed on June 3, July 8, and November 10. Would you like the shipping quantities for all three orders?

CALLER: Yes, please.

YOU: I'm typing in the request for the June 3 quantity. It should be up in just a second. There it is. That quantity was . . .

And so forth.

Your objective is to avoid dead air, which creates anxiety in the caller, who worries she has been cut off or has been forgotten. Banish dead air by emulating an old-fashioned radio sportscaster. Provide a blow-by-blow narrative account of your actions as you perform them.

TRANSFERRING A CALL

Taking ownership of a call does not mean you cannot transfer the call if doing so is necessary to address the customer's issue. There are plenty of good reasons for transferring a call. A colleague in another department may be better equipped to handle the customer's question or request. The caller may have reached you instead of the person or department he meant to call. You may simply be unable to answer the caller's question, but you know a colleague who can. Even though you may have a compelling reason to make the transfer, think of your responsibility as not merely handing off the call, but *selling* it. After all, you own it.

Begin by securing permission to place the caller on hold while you identify and then brief the colleague to whom you intend to sell the call. If you either anticipate or discover that locating and briefing the colleague will take some time, arrange to return the caller's call. Don't keep him on interminable hold. Be certain that you set a specific time for the return call. Once you do have the colleague on the line, brief her by supplying the name of the caller, the nature of his question, issue, or problem, and what it is the caller wants. You should never hand off the call without supplying all the key information. Delivering excellent customer service means never putting the caller in the position of having to repeat himself.

Should the colleague you have identified to take the call tell you that she cannot provide the needed help, ask her for advice on whom to consult next. After obtaining this advice, return to your caller (if you have placed him on hold) and ask permission to keep him on hold longer while you consult the other colleague. Alternatively, agree on a time for you to call back. Even though you yourself may be frustrated, keep this new development in a positive frame:

> **YOU:** I've just spoken to Jane Barnes, one of our technicians, who recommended that we consult Claire Morehead, who is one of our engineers. It will take me, oh, three minutes or so to get hold of Claire. May I put you on hold for that time, or would you prefer that I call you back?

Do not imply that the first colleague you tried *failed* to provide an answer. Give the caller the message that she, in fact, made a valuable recommendation, which you are following.

WORDS AND PHRASES TO USE

A few minutes

Expedite

Facilitate

Good afternoon/evening/morning

How may I help you?

I can help you with that

I need to consult/get some information

I'm sorry you are having that difficulty

It is a pleasure

Let me quickly research that for you

Let's get you on your way

May I put you on hold for X minutes?

Now I understand

Quickly

Thank you for your help/patience/ understanding

This is a common issue

Up and running

We can resolve this

WORDS AND PHRASES TO AVOID

Calm down

Hold on

I can't find anybody who knows anything about this

I can't understand you

I don't know what to tell you

I'm putting you on hold

If the call gets lost, just call back

Nothing we can do about that

Oh, that's a tough one

Please call us back later

This may take some time

Try again later

We'll get to this as soon as we can

Well, that's our policy

You should have called earlier

You're not in our system

You've made a mistake

BY EMAIL

Although most customer service transactions take place on the telephone, email is as important in customer service as it is in most other areas of modern business communication.

The Email Challenge

If you are responsible for cleaning your own house or apartment, doubtless you are thankful for such modern conveniences as the vacuum cleaner, dishwasher, clothes washer, dryer, and so on. After all, these "labor-saving devices" clean more thoroughly, efficiently, and quickly than the broom, mop, and sink of old.

Right, yes?

Actually, yes *and* no.

Our modern "labor-saving devices" have raised the standards by which we judge a clean house. Back in the day, "clean" was defined by what a broom could do. Today, "clean" is defined as a meticulously vacuumed house. While a vacuum cleaner can get a house "broom clean" faster than a broom can, a broom will probably get the same space broom clean faster than a vacuum will get it "vacuum cleaner clean." It is quite possible that, by raising expectations, our labor-saving arsenal may have created more, not less, work.

Something of the same sort is true of email. The technology that makes it easy for us to reach out to one another also invites more messages and demands more—and quicker—replies. True, you no longer have to dig out stationery and load it in a printer every time you want to write a message. You don't have to address an email the way you have to address a paper letter. You don't have to get an envelope, fold the letter, seal the envelope, and affix a stamp. Much of the time, you don't even have to look up an address, especially if you are replying to a message.

A lot of time and labor is saved, but the availability of email generates many more messages to you, together with the expectation of a reply—and a reply sooner rather than later. Not only does email technology create at least as much labor as it saves, it heaps a fair amount of pressure on each of us. The very speed and ready accessibility of email communication that saves us so much time also places demands on our time.

Take a Breath, Give Some Thought

The greatest liability inherent in email is its very ease. Typically, we think harder before we pick up the phone to make a call than we do when we send an email. Not only are most emails dashed off in one draft, we often don't even read over the message before clicking "Send." If, as writing teachers tell us, the writing that can be read the fastest and the easiest takes the most time and the greatest pains to create, it must also be true that what is dashed off hurriedly must be the hardest for a reader to decipher. In other words, when you rush through writing an email, you may be forcing the reader to put in the time you failed to invest. If that reader is a customer, you are committing the customer service sin of creating rather than solving problems.

The most effective thing you can do to increase the clarity and impact of your email communications is to take a breath and think before you touch the keyboard, then read over what you have written before you click on "Send." Approach email as you would approach any other important business communication. Failure to do this may create a poor impression on your correspondent; may create resentment from a reader who doesn't appreciate struggling with your message; may create misunderstanding, which could be costly.

The ease of email tempts action before thought. Don't feel obligated to answer emails instantly, or to send off your own very first thought. Regard your message as a first draft. Delay sending it until you have reread it and edited it as necessary.

Who Should Go into the Loop?

In the days of paper communication, sending "cc" copies—carbon copies or courtesy copies—used to require real work. You had to duplicate paper memos, writing in each recipient's name. Because it took work, it was used only when truly necessary. With email, however, sending a single message to multiple recipients amounts to nothing more than a few extra mouse clicks. The result is a lot of unwanted messages sent to a lot of people.

Curbing cc's is a major stride toward cutting down on email overload. Agree on a cc list for routine customer service emails and adhere to it. In general:

■ Copy anyone who, according to company procedures or policies, must receive a copy.

- In addition, copy all those who will be in any way affected by the content of the message.
- If the message concerns a particular project or product line, consider copying key members of the team responsible for the project or product line.

Headers

An email begins with a *header*, which typically consists of:

The subject of the message
The sender
The date and time sent
The addressee(s)

Most email programs also include an indication if an attachment is present. Some put the actual attachment at the head of the message, some at the end.

Always fill in the subject line. Many senders neglect to do this, thereby making it difficult for the recipient to sort through received emails and decide whether to read the email now, later, or at all. Failing to include a subject line is not only rude, it invites being ignored or simply overlooked. The best strategy is to make use of the subject line to write something that is both informative and provocative.

Think about that word, *provocative*. The action you want to *provoke* with your subject line is a prompt and careful reading of the substance of the message in the body of the email. You have to *sell* ideas and information to your correspondents much as you might sell them products and services. Open with a statement that commands attention by appealing to your correspondent's needs. For example, you might give the subject of an email on new ordering procedures the title "New ordering procedures" or even "Important new ordering procedures." If you really want your correspondent to read the email, however, try something like this: "How to get your order faster" or "Get your order faster!"

The header content is pretty standard on all email programs. Many programs also provide the option of adding a signature as well. This is not a script signature, but a collection of information that automatically appears at the bottom of any email message the sender transmits:

John Doe, Sales Manager
jdoe@widget.com
Widget Wonders Inc.
1234 W. 5th Street
Anyplace, NY 12340
Phone: 555-555-5555

If your email software doesn't provide a signature, you can create a copy-and-paste file with important contact information. A good "signature" will save you from having to repeat innumerable keystrokes.

A Matter of Personality

A lot of people equate email correspondence more closely with verbal conversation than with paper memos or letters. For this reason, there is not only room for personality in emails, but the expectation of it.

In email communication, informality is both expected and tolerated to a greater degree than in telephone conversation and to a *much* greater degree than in paper business letters. This is no excuse to be sloppy, however. Although spelling and punctuation errors are more readily forgiven in email than in other written correspondence, take the time to proofread and correct yourself. If your email messages seem both spontaneous *and* correct in grammar and spelling, you will appear intelligent and caring.

Beware of Big Brother

Any message you send to a customer becomes a business record. Compose your messages with this in mind. Be aware that numerous decisions in court cases have upheld an employer's absolute right to monitor all email going in and out of the network and equipment the employer owns or controls. In fact, all email generated by employees on employer-owned or employer-controlled equipment is considered the sole and exclusive property of the employer. Always assume that everything you send and receive via the company's email system is being read by management.

In addition to ensuring that your email correspondence to customers is pleasantly businesslike, observe the following rules:

- Do not use the company's email system to send personal messages.
- Do not use the company's email system to conduct non-company business (such as freelance work).
- Do not write anything you would not want your boss to read.

Keep a Copy of Everything

Make certain that you retain copies of all emails sent and received. Use the "archive" function of your email program or follow any protocols your employer specifies. Emails are business records. Do not delete them.

CHAPTER 15

Sell Up, Sell Right

Traditionally, Customer Service has been thought of as a back-office operation—strictly a support service and something the company is obligated to take on. Unlike Sales, it has not always been seen as a profit producer.

While some traditions are worth upholding and perpetuating, others are worth revisiting, revising, and even discarding. The emerging view of Customer Service does discard this traditional view and sees it instead as seamlessly connected with Sales. In progressive companies, service has become proactive. It reaches out to prospects as well as to current customers to promote the "service advantage" as a key product feature, and it also works with established customers to sell additional products and offer additional value.

START BY SELLING THE SERVICE ADVANTAGE

Make no mistake, Customer Service is the go-to resource for people with problems and complaints, but it should also be the go-to source for information and education about the value your company offers its customers. The emails that follow in this section are intended to be sent to prospects and new customers. They are designed to prompt them to think beyond a particular piece of merchandise and consider the dimension of service behind it. Your objective is to persuade the prospect or customer to think about customer service in a new way. Put the emphasis on service, on accountability, and on collaboration and partnership.

EXAMPLES

Introducing Customer Service

Subject: Discover the service difference

Dear John Williams,

Thank you for visiting the XYZ Company website. I know you came to see our standout line of products, but great technology is not all we offer. XYZ has an award-winning Customer Service Department, and you should know about it before you make your purchasing decision.

A lot of companies think "Customer Service Department" is just a polite term for "Complaint Department." For that reason, they hope you never call. Well, that's not the way we do things at XYZ.

Of course, we're here for you if you have a problem with any of our products. But we're here for you when things are going just fine, too. Our job is not only to fix things, it's also to make our products give you the greatest value every time you use them. That's why we offer:

- A Priority Customer Answer Line—for all your questions about our products.
- Expedited Accessory Service—for all your accessory needs.
- DIY Helper—your sources for spare parts, upgrades, and complete instructions so that DIY doesn't mean you have to DIY all by yourself.
- XYZ Idea Place—a website you can visit to share your ideas about how we can serve you better.

When you buy an XYZ product you don't just buy great technology, you buy our commitment to great service.

Hope to hear from you soon!

A. J. Sparks
Customer Service Director
XYZ Company
xyz.com
555-555-5555

Subject: Don't overlook value

Dear Ben Johnson:

Welcome to the XYZ family!

I'm confident that you are still discovering all the great benefits of your new widget, but I bet you've overlooked one very important benefit. And no wonder. You can't see it until you actually need it.

Our Customer Service and Tech Support Department has won every major industry award for five years running. We're proud of it, and we put as much thought, planning, and imagination into our service as we put into our products.

See for yourself. Visit us at xyz.com/service. Take a tour of our full program of tech support, including our Interactive Interlocutor, which is designed to get you answers to your technical questions in record-breaking time.

If you need more than an online resource, our technical representatives are available 24/7 to talk you through any installation, configuration, or operation situation. Our Customer Service representatives work the same hours, and they are ready to help you with answers to your questions about upgrades, accessories, service contracts, and training seminars.

Give this key product benefit a try. Come visit us at xyz.xyz/service today.

Sincerely,
Mary Moll
Service Coordinator

XYZ Company
xyz.com/service
555-555-5555

What Makes You Special

Consider promoting Customer Service as the ownership benefit that sets you apart and above the competition.

Subject: Meet Customer Service

Dear Sam Browne:

We have a lot of competition. But we assume you know that, since you obviously have been thinking of investing in a new widget. We also assume that you've reached the conclusion that most of the widgets out there work reasonably well. They all get the job done.

That is, until they don't.

And when your widget quits on you—or when you simply have a question about your machine—you will discover just what sets us apart from our competitors. It's not a difference in our materials and technology. It is a difference in our people.

We want you to know that when you buy an XYZ product, you buy more than the best hardware. You buy great service—service our competitors cannot match. We recruit our Customer Support staff from the ranks of the foremost consultants in the industry, and we devote an unprecedented 20 percent of our corporate resources to ensuring that Customer Support maintains excellence at all levels.

Our Customer Support staff not only rides to the rescue when you have a problem, they will help you avoid problems in the first place with our Installation Service Line.

They will help you maximize your range of applications with our Imagination Line.

They will advise you on accessories and related products—ours as well as those from other manufacturers—through our Equipment Line.

Please, check out the XYZ difference at xyz.com/service today. Or call 555-555-5555 to speak to a representative.

Sincerely,
Pat Moran
CTO, Service
XYZ Company
xyz.com/service
555-555-5555

Premium Service Offer

Many companies offer fee-based "premium" service plans. These are high-value products that can generate significant profits and therefore deserve promotion.

Subject: Introducing your Personal Service Advantage

Dear Max Bruch:

Please take a moment to consider the Personal Service Advantage.

You rely on your Model 123 Widget to maintain a consistent level of high-quality production. You can't afford downtime, and neither can the customers who count on you. That's why we want you to know about the Personal Service Advantage. It is as simple as it is vital to ensuring uninterrupted service from your Model 123.

We **guarantee** that when you call or message us any weekday between 6:30 a.m. and 10 p.m., you will be connected to a Model 123–qualified technical consultant within three minutes. We **guarantee** that the technician you speak to will have instant access to your complete and up-to-date service record. We **guarantee** that the technician will have the answers you need and will have the authority to dispatch service personnel to your location within two hours, max.

Our products rarely falter. When they do, the Personal Service Advantage gets them up and running as fast as possible. Rely on it.

Call 555-555-5555 or go online at xyz.com/PSA to get the Personal Service Advantage—right now.

Sincerely yours,
Paul Brown
Director of Service
XYZ Company
xyz.com/PSA
555-555-5555

WORDS AND PHRASES TO USE

A real convenience
A snap
A speedy and simplified
   approach
Always ready when you are
Call 24 hours a day
Complete confidence
Easy access
Eliminates worry
Enhances performance
Give us a call
Goes the distance
Has never been easier

Here for you
Kiss your hassles good-bye
Let us come to the rescue
Makes your life easier
No problem!
Peace of mind
Quick access
Service
There is no easier way
Total confidence/
   satisfaction
We'll take it from here
Whenever you need us

WORDS AND PHRASES TO AVOID

As time permits
Before you call
Call early before we get busy
Do our best
If we can't fix it, nobody can
Make an appointment
Next available
Required

Sorry for the delay/the
   inconvenience
You must have the following
   information
You need to
Your responsibility

SELLING FROM A SERVICE PERSPECTIVE

Each time a customer calls for service, you have an opportunity to make a sale. In the case of many product lines, it is actually the Customer Service representative who is in the most advantageous position to promote accessories and upgrades. The customer support professional occupies a singularly knowledgeable position from which to make authoritative and genuinely valuable recommendations.

The email messages that follow promote merchandise related to a product a customer has recently purchased from the sender. It is key to the selling strategy to preserve your credibility as a provider of customer *support*. Customers want to feel that your primary job is to support them, not to sell them an endless array of merchandise. For this reason, avoid hard-sell tactics. Make no claim of presenting a "once-in-a-lifetime offer" or an "absolute must-have." Above all else, your tone should be informational, albeit within the framework of a basic sales presentation.

Begin by establishing the credible need for accessories or related products. Typically, the basis of this need will be the enhancement or protection of the initial investment in the original product. Next, present the benefits of the merchandise offered. How will it build on the value of the product the customer already owns?

Ask for questions. If this elicits objections, answer them. The most effective approach puts the emphasis on the cost-effectiveness of the product.

Finally, as with any sale, move the customer to act. Close the communication by telling your customer how to place an order or how to obtain additional information.

EXAMPLES

Products Related to a Customer's Recent Purchase

Few customers find value in an advertisement, but everyone can use information. Offer the value of product news:

Subject: Important information about your new XYZ Widget

Dear Mr. Clarkson:

We at XYZ thought you would want to know about the following new products now available to owners of the XYZ Widget:

- <Product 1> is a great add-on to your widget. By allowing you to <describe operation>, this accessory is a great way to make the most of a wise investment.
- <Product 2> is for users who need expanded <describe> capability. With <Product 2>, you can customize the output from your widget in the following ways: <list>
- <Product 3> is for those who want the added flexibility of operating on house current, rechargeable batteries, or their automobile battery. This cost-effective option greatly expands the utility of your widget. And, yes, we carry a full line of rechargeable batteries.

Click on this <link> to log on to our website, where you will find full specs for these and other fine accessories. If you need help and advice, give us a call at 555-555-5555. We're here for you.

Sincerely,
XYZ Service Team
xyz.com/service
555-555-5555

Spare Part Advisory of Availability

Keep your customer informed on an ongoing basis about products relating to merchandise she has purchased from you in the past.

Subject: Service advisory from XYZ Company

Dear Ms. Petersen:

Because you are someone who has ordered <accessory> in the past, we thought you would want to know that as of <date>, this item will be discontinued, and we will stop carrying it as soon as our present stock is exhausted. If you are planning to purchase this <accessory> again, we suggest you do so before <date> to ensure its availability. You can order directly by clicking on this link.

For your information, <accessory> is being replaced by <accessory 2>, an enhanced product that includes the following features you won't find on <accessory>: <list>. You may therefore want to consider ordering <accessory 2> instead of <accessory>. Just click on this link: <link>.

If you would like more information about either item, please give us a call at 555-555-5555.

Sincerely,
Peter Winger
Service Associate
XYZ Company
xyz.com/service
555-555-5555

Phone Call Recommending Accessories

CALLER: My name is Shirley Francis, and I am trying to figure out what <accessory> would be best for my <product>. I am looking to use the <product> to <description of use>.

YOU: I can help you with that, Ms. Francis. We have two attachments available that will convert your <product> into a highly efficient <type of device>. The first, <product 1>, will allow you to perform the following operations: <list>. The second, <product 2>, performs these functions in addition: <list>. So if these additional functions are important to you, you will want to buy <product 2>. If not, you may want to choose <product 1>, which is priced significantly lower, at

$XX, whereas <product 2> is priced at $XX. But if the additional functionality is important to you, <product 2> represents a particularly good value.

Precedent-Based Upselling

A persuasive approach to upselling current customers is to cite as a precedent the purchases others have made. A simple email is sufficient to get your customer thinking:

Subject: How to add value to your new purchase

Dear Mary Lou Edmunds:

Thank you for recently purchasing <product 1>. It has been our experience that customers who use <product 1> are very serious about <type of application>. For this reason, I thought I would take a moment of your time to tell you about <product 2>. Used with <product 1>, it will take care of all your <type of application> needs and is the most advanced and economical approach available today.

If you would like to learn more or place an order, just click on this link: <link>. And if you have any questions, please call me directly at 555-555-5555.

Sincerely,
S. G. Arnold
Service Adviser
XYZ Company
zyz.com/service
555-555-5555

Upselling to an Extended Service Contract

Many products come with a limited warranty only, which creates an opportunity for upselling the customer to a fee-based extended service contract. This is a lucrative sales area, and it also offers a significant benefit to the customer; however, many customers are suspicious of extended service contract offers. There is also the danger of implying that the product purchased from you is sufficiently imperfect or unreliable to *require* a fee-based extension.

Put the emphasis on the benefits of the extended service contract, which include time saved and peace of mind gained.

Subject: Purchase peace of mind today

Dear Mr. Smith:

I have a problem. My company manufactures the finest, most durable widget available today. Now I want to tell you about an extended service contract to fix it if something goes wrong. Naturally, this will suggest to you one of two possibilities: either I'm trying to sell you something you really don't need, or I'm expecting your widget to break.

Well, neither of these "possibilities" applies in your case. What you should know, however, is that even the best widgets require regular maintenance, and even with proper maintenance, the use they get is typically hard and demanding. Let's face it, eventual malfunction is a possibility. Now, your warranty does cover all defects for the first <time period> of ownership, but it does not pay for regular maintenance or for anything that might go wrong after the warranty expires on <date of expiration>.

With private technical contractors charging $XX for major maintenance, and repairs averaging $XX per call, it doesn't take a rocket scientist to figure out that the $XX per <time period> you pay for our <time period> extended service contract is money well invested.

The maintenance we offer will help to ensure that your widget will give you superb service for years to come. The extension of warranty coverage gives you peace of mind when it comes to controlling possible future repair costs and keeping downtime to an absolute minimum.

Let me say more about this second point. As a holder of our extended service contract, you are automatically enrolled on our "A List." This means that nobody on the other end of a phone is *ever* going to tell you that they'll "try to squeeze you in" a week from next Tuesday. Our service contract guarantees a service call within twenty-four hours. Usually, we can reach you on the same day that you call.

Finally: Our extended service contract entitles you to very special discount prices on equipment loaners—for those rare times when we cannot fix the problem on-site.

Please take note that you must order the extended service contract by <date>. To order, click on this link, <link>, or call me, Ed Johnson, at 555-555-5555.

Sincerely,
Ed Johnson
Contract Service
XYZ Company
xyz.com/contract service
555-555-5555

Special Offers

Special offers are a natural sales path for current customers to take. Emphasize the exclusivity of the offer—the fact that the customer qualifies for a special value precisely because she *is* a current customer. Special offers not only mean sales. They build rapport and loyalty.

Subject: An exclusive special offer for you

Dear Alexandra Morris:

As a user of <product>, you'll want to know about our new limited-availability special offers on some of the most popular accessories that will greatly enhance your enjoyment of <product>. Please take a moment to click on the link below, which will show you a range of accessories that are now available now at very special prices.

May I suggest that you look very closely at <accessory 1> and <accessory 2>. These are top sellers among owners of <product> like you. Prices on these items have never been lower.

Sincerely yours,
The XYZ Customer Service Team
xyz.com/special offer
555-555-5555

WORDS AND PHRASES TO USE

A mouse click/phone call away   Just ask

Absolute confidence   Let us help you

Added value   No matter what you need

Assurance   Online scheduling

Continuing assistance   Peace of mind

Custom service   Protect your investment

Customized for you   Takes the guesswork out of

Enhance the value   service

Extend   Total confidence

Flexibility   We deliver

Full-service shop   We keep our promises

Guaranteed/incomparable/   We stand behind you

    individualized service   We won't let you down

WORDS AND PHRASES TO AVOID

Always perfect   Never

Don't be left on your own   Position in line

Don't lose out   Unlikely

Give us a try   When disaster strikes

Minimal hold times   You may never need it

UPSELLING WITHOUT UPSETTING

Customer Service representatives are in an ideal position to recommend products and services related to merchandise an existing customer has already purchased. The selling scenario is slightly more complicated when it comes to what might be called *direct* upselling—that is, offering a customer an upgrade to a product she owns. The strategy here is to present and promote the upgrade without denigrating the original product.

Present the upgrade as an evolutionary step beyond the original product. Frame the decision to upgrade constructively, as logically building on the original purchase.

EXAMPLES

Subject: Special upgrade opportunity

Dear Marion Morrison:

I am excited to tell you about an exclusive offer to owners of the Model 1600. As you undoubtedly know, the Model 1600 has been praised by industry insiders and professional consultants since it was first introduced five years ago. The leading national consumer polling agency has consistently placed it in the top rank of customer satisfaction. Clearly, you made a wise purchase when you chose it.

You now have an opportunity to trade it in and move up to the next step in the evolution the Model 1600 started.

The new Model 1700 packs all the features and benefits you have been enjoying, plus these: <list>. It is, in short, easier to use, more powerful, and more flexible. It is the future of <type of product> products.

And because you've already made a commitment to the <product> idea with the Model 1600, we are offering you the Model 1700 at the special upgrade price of only $XXX. That is XX percent off the full price of the product.

What's more, you have the opportunity to upgrade before the Model 1700 is released to the general public on <date>. Let us welcome you to the future, and let us reward you with this special offer. Please click on the link below for more information or to order today.

Sincerely yours,
Model 1600 Upgrade Team
xyz.com/upgrade
555-555-5555

WORDS AND PHRASES TO USE

A new benchmark/dimension
Ahead of the curve
At last it's here!

Based on your suggestions
Better than ever
Brand-new

Change is good/very good

Enhanced

Enriched

Even better

Evolutionary

Exciting

Exclusive

Extended

Groundbreaking
design

Here it is!

Innovative

Latest technology

New opportunity

Reinvented

Revolutionary

Stay ahead of the curve

Step up

The next logical step

Trade in

Update

Upgrade

We make things better

We reinvented the <product>

We're pleased to announce/
offer

WORDS AND PHRASES TO AVOID

Don't get left behind

Don't get stuck

Fad

Follow the leader

It's that time again

Latest sensation

Old

Replaces

The latest thing

Tired

Trade-up time

Worn out

CHAPTER 16

Provide Support

Even these days, when it is expected to contribute to the bottom line by extending and enhancing the sales function, the principal focus of the Customer Service Department is to support existing customers. This chapter is about "how to say it" to provide optimum customer support.

LISTEN UP

As we have said repeatedly, great customer service begins with effective listening. Not only are acute listening skills crucial to solving the customer's problems and addressing his wants and needs, they also provide proof to the customer that you and your organization believe he is important and that you value what he is saying to you.

Understand that *listening* is not the same as *hearing*. Good hearing is a matter of physiology, neurology, and auditory physics. Good listening, however, is a skill. It can be learned, developed, and improved through practice. Listen. Make a point of listening for comprehension. Spend a half hour each day listening to news on the radio—not the television, the radio. Focus on it.

Make an effort to comprehend it. You might even want to make notes. Repeat this exercise every day for a month, and you will emerge a better listener than you are today.

Make a conscious effort to develop the following five habits of effective listening:

1. *Be present.* While listening, listen. Don't think about what you are going to say when it's your turn. Don't worry if you do not have the answer the other person is seeking. (Answers are important, but what your customer wants most from you is simply to be heard and understood.) During the time the other person is talking, you should do nothing but listen.

2. *Allow no interruptions.* When you are on the telephone, it is very tempting to multitask—attend to something on your computer, read correspondence, and so on. Allow no one and nothing to distract you from listening.

3. *Restrain your emotions.* Anger and irritation are like a fog that gets between you and your caller. If the caller says something that disturbs you or that cries out to be refuted, restrain yourself. Your job is to listen. Hear the other person out.

4. *Refuse to assume superior knowledge.* If you feel dismissive toward the caller's message, you cannot really listen to it. Do not assume you know better than your caller. Do not allow a prematurely formulated answer to block you from actually listening to what the caller has to say.

5. *Don't fool yourself into believing you are listening when you are not.* Just sitting with a headset on does not mean you are listening. Be honest with your caller and with yourself. If you find yourself drifting into inattention, apologize and ask the caller to repeat.

START ASKING QUESTIONS

When you learn to listen effectively, you will discover that many callers know exactly what they want, and you will also discover that many more do not.

The fact is that many who call Customer Service are not fully sure of what they want or need. Help them to find out by asking questions.

Get the Basic Background

A customer calls because his brand-new widget is not working as promised. That is the reason for his call. That is what is uppermost in his mind. Before you can help him—or transfer his call to someone who can help—you need to fill in such background information as the caller's name and address, the serial number of the product, and so on. Politely interrupt:

> "I'm sorry you are having a problem. So that we can thoroughly resolve these issues quickly, please let me get some background information. First, may I have your first and last name?"

Then continue to acquire all the background information you need. Preface these questions by making them part of the process of providing help—"So that we can thoroughly resolve these issues quickly"—will make the caller calmer, more confident, and more cooperative.

Probe

Use probing questions to gather the substance of the caller's issue quickly and clearly. Emulate the old-time newspaper journalist and ask questions about *who*, *what*, *when*, *where*, and *why*. Open-ended questions will yield more detail than a mere yes or no.

What is the nature of the problem?
What happens when you <do something>?
Does this happen every time you <do something>?
When does this happen?
After <event> happened, what happened next?
You say that your unit does <quote customer>. Can you give me an
   example of this?
How long has this been a problem?

Confirm

To ensure that you understand your caller's issues, mirror what he tells you. You can do this by asking confirming questions. For instance:

Let me make sure I understand. What you are saying is . . .
Is my understanding accurate?
Do I understand you correctly?
Did I miss anything in my explanation?
Do you feel I understand the problem?
Is there anything else I need to know?
Does the solution I suggest seem helpful to you?
How do you feel about my suggestion?
Is this solution satisfactory?

WALK THE CALLER THROUGH IT

Providing telephone support can be highly demanding. In trying to work through a problem or procedure with a caller, you obviously cannot see what's going on. You therefore have to go out of your way to ensure that you have a full and complete picture of all the issues. This can be frustrating and fatiguing. Well, no one said that customer service is easy.

Ask comprehensive questions, so that you can be certain your perception of the problem is accurate and complete. Use the caller as your eyes. Ask her to report to you on what she sees happening.

Suppose a customer calls and tells you that she "can't get the widget to work":

YOU: Is the unit turned on now?
CALLER: Oh, yes.
YOU: What is it doing now?
CALLER: Nothing.
YOU: Let's see if I can help. To do so, I need some information. May I have your name please? Also, could you please give me the serial number of the unit?

CALLER: [*Supplies information.*]

YOU: Great. Now I can pull up the files and specifications of your unit on my computer screen. I will also be keeping notes on our conversation today. It will take just about thirty seconds for the information to come up on my screen . . . It's been very hot here in Chicago. How's the weather where you are?

CALLER: Not too bad here . . .

YOU: Good . . . Ah, here's your information. I'm now looking at the data, so let's get into your specific situation. Now, since we're on the phone, I need your help to get me oriented exactly to your situation. So forgive me if I start at the very beginning. Have you confirmed that power is getting to the unit?

CALLER: I'm not sure what you mean. All I know is that the thing isn't working.

YOU: I understand. So please help me check a few basic items to narrow down the problem. Look around at the back of the unit. Is it plugged into a standard wall outlet?

CALLER: Sure it is.

YOU: There are no indicator lights on?

CALLER: No. It's dead.

YOU: Then let's just make sure we have *correct* power into the unit. Perhaps we tripped a breaker. This has happened before. Could you plug in any other another appliance—a lamp, an electric clock, or anything— into the same outlet and confirm that we are receiving power?

CALLER: Okay. [*Does it.*] Wow! The power is off at the outlet!

YOU: Well, that's important information. Do you detect any burning odors anywhere around the unit?

CALLER: No, no. Nothing like that.

YOU: Do you see any oil or signs of anything leaking anywhere on the control panel? Spilled coffee, maybe? Please look carefully. We don't want things to get any worse.

CALLER: No, nothing of the kind.

YOU: Feel the control panel surface and the sides of the unit. Are they hot? Normally, they will be warm, but not hot.

CALLER: No. They are neither warm nor hot. The unit is just dead.

YOU: Our problem may be elsewhere, then. Let's investigate. Please turn the "on/off" switch to the off position. Now, do you have access to the circuit breakers in your office?

CALLER: Yes.

YOU: Please go to the breaker box and reset any breaker that has tripped. I'll hold on while you do that. Take all the time you need.

CALLER: Okay. [*Returns.*] Yes, it *was* tripped. I reset it.

YOU: Thanks! Now, let's see if we can get the unit running again. We'll need to turn it on.

CALLER: Look, I don't want to get a shock or start a fire or anything . . .

YOU: Don't worry. The worst that can happen is that the circuit breaker will trip again. If it does, it will do so immediately. You might even hear a popping noise as it trips. And if it does trip, we'll just have to dispatch a technician to your location. So go ahead and turn the widget on. You'll be just fine.

CALLER: Okay. Huh! It's coming online. I don't see anything unusual happening.

YOU: What does your LCD display show?

CALLER: Just that the unit is on. Nothing unusual. It looks like it always does.

YOU: Good. Let's just run a few tests together, okay?

CALLER: I've never done that before.

YOU: That's okay. Don't worry. We'll work on this together until we both get it. I'll walk you through the procedure every step of the way. It's no big deal, anyway. We may discover a problem, but nothing we do can cause a new one. Okay then. Let's start with the first test. Using the keys below the LCD screen, punch in the command <command>.

CALLER: Done. Now what?

YOU: Look at the LCD. It should say "Running Test."

CALLER: It does.

YOU: Great. This test will allow us to check <list items>. If this test confirms that there are no problems, we will run a second test together. It will tell us . . .

WORDS AND PHRASES TO USE

Answer

Assist

Clear up

Help

I completely understand

I'll be right here

I'll stay on the line

I've seen this before

Leave it to me

Let's move on to the next step

Let's try this together

Not unusual

Now I see

Perfectly safe

Resolve

Safety

Solution/solve

Take care of that for you

Terrific

Thank you

This has happened before

Understand

Up and running

Walk you through

We need to investigate

We will do it together

You will be fine

You're doing very well

WORDS AND PHRASES TO AVOID

Fault

Give it a shot

Have you ever read the manual?

Here goes nuthin'

I don't know what your
problem is

I give up

I just don't understand

Let's go over it *again*

Mistake

Move a little faster, please

Take a chance

This is simple

Uncharted waters

Why are you taking so long?

You need to read the manual

Your fault

OWN THE CALLER'S PROBLEM

Remember the *call* ownership concept we discussed in Chapter 14? The concept of ownership can also be applied to your caller's *problem*. Once you engage a caller's issue, you own it. You might not be able to resolve it personally, but you cannot abandon it. If you can't fix the problem yourself, during the call, you must set the caller on a course toward resolution. When something goes wrong with a technology they do not understand, many callers become quite anxious as well as frustrated. In these cases, it is especially important that you take ownership of the problem. Provide your absolute assurance of help.

YOU: [*Picks up phone. Greets caller and identifies self.*] How may I help you?

CALLER: I own <product> and just can't get the damn thing to work.

YOU: Let's see what's happening. First, so that I can help you, I need some information. May I have your name please? And could you please give me the serial number of the unit?

CALLER: [*Supplies information.*]

YOU: Thank you. This lets me pull up the information I need on my computer screen. I'll also take notes on our conversation today. Okay. I've got the information up. Now tell me, what is the unit currently doing?

CALLER: Nothing!

YOU: So did it just quit on you? Have you ever had it up and running?

CALLER: Actually, no. I don't really know what to do.

YOU: I'm sure we can help. The unit is designed to be very user-friendly. So let's just get into it together and get you up and running right away. Look for the switch in the upper right-hand corner of the control panel. Turn it on.

CALLER: I don't want to break anything . . .

YOU: You won't, don't worry. I'll walk you through this, one step at a time. Just follow my instructions and report what happens. Go ahead and flip on the switch and tell me what happens.

CALLER: Oh, the monitor is coming on. It's showing a bunch of codes. Is something wrong?

YOU: Well, why don't you just read the codes to me. That will tell us.

CALLER: [*Reads.*]

YOU: Perfectly normal. The codes you are seeing should be on the screen at this point. So let's take the next step. I'd like you to press the F1 key, which will bring up a manual in the upper right corner of your screen.

CALLER: Why do I need the manual?

YOU: I would like to review how and where some procedures are documented for you in the on-screen manual. This way, in the future, you won't have to spend your time calling on an issue you can resolve more quickly yourself.

CALLER: Okay. I've got the manual up. What next?

YOU: Go to page five. There you will see the meaning of all the codes that are on your screen. Now, let's review the startup sequence together. The first code means <description>. The second code means <description> . . .

WORDS AND PHRASES TO USE

Designed to be user friendly

Did I leave you with any unanswered questions?

Do you have any concerns/questions?

I know the feeling

I understand

I'll help you

I'll wait

Let's make sure everything's okay/you are satisfied

Let's work together on this

Take all the time you need

Tell me what you see

We can fix this together

You can do it

You can't make it worse

You will be up and running shortly

You won't break anything

WORDS AND PHRASES TO AVOID

Don't be silly

I'll tell you just once

It's a cinch

Listen to me this time

Man up!

Most customers don't have a hard time like this

No reason to feel scared

No reason to worry

Nothing to it

Stop worrying

You really should be able to do this

You shouldn't feel intimidated

FOLLOW-UP STRATEGIES

Ownership of your customer's problems, concerns, and issues can be productively extended beyond one particular call to Customer Service. Demonstrate your commitment to total customer satisfaction by developing a strategy for diligent and courteous follow up. Within two or three days of the customer's call, either send an email or make a phone call to follow-up with the customer.

EXAMPLES

Follow-up Email

Subject: Service follow-up from XYZ Company

Dear Jane Archer:

I'm writing to follow up on our conversation on <date> about your issue with <product name>. When we concluded our call, you were up and running, and everything seemed to be working satisfactorily. I wanted to make sure that all is still well and that I left none of your questions and concerns unaddressed.

Please reply to this email if there is anything further I can help you with. Your total satisfaction is our goal.

It was a pleasure speaking with you.

Sincerely,
Peter Wall
Customer Service Representative
XYZ Company
xyz.com
555-555-5555

Follow-up Phone Call

YOU: Ms. Archer, this is Pete Wall at XYZ Customer Service. How are you this morning?

CUSTOMER: I'm good.

YOU: I was calling to follow up on our conversation last week about your <product>. I wanted to make certain that you were up and running and that everything was now satisfactory. Everything going smoothly now?

CUSTOMER: Yes, thank you.

YOU: I'm glad to hear that—and it's what I expected to hear. Just to re-mind you, in the future, if you ever get an Error Code 234 message again, try hitting the reset button. Nine times out of ten, that resolves the issue—and saves you the trouble of a call to us. Before I leave you to the rest of your morning, is there anything else I can help you with? Any questions I left unanswered?

CUSTOMER: No. I'm good.

YOU: Wonderful. Have a great day!

WORDS AND PHRASES TO USE

A pleasure

Call anytime

Calling to
 follow up

Complete
 satisfaction

Confirm that

Ensure

Happy

I wanted to check in and make
 sure everything is now
 running smoothly

Make certain

No more problems

Resolved

Service

Totally satisfied

Unanswered

WORDS AND PHRASES TO AVOID

Don't want any surprises
 from you

Don't want to hear from
 you again

Don't want you to complain again

Don't want you to sue us

Not sure we fixed the
 problem

Please certify that you have no
 more problems

CHAPTER 17

Welcome All Complaints
(and Ask for More!)

Back in the day, "Customer Service" was called the "Complaint Department." It must not have been a very pleasant place to work, which may be one reason why the name was changed. No matter, many who today work in "Customer Service" still *think* of themselves as staffing a "Complaint Department." So let's consider yet another name change—this one from *Complaint Department* to *Opportunity Department*.

THE BIGGER THE COMPLAINT, THE BIGGER
THE OPPORTUNITY

There's a name for a person who *wants* things to go wrong. In polite company, the word is *sociopath*, but maybe *real jerk* is more to the point. Nevertheless, you can count on it: Things *do* go wrong. So why not figure out a way to make the most out of the inevitable snafus? Turn each of them into an opportunity to give exceptional service and thereby create a satisfied customer.

No question, when Sarah's widget dies a premature death, she will call you in a very bad mood. It will get much worse, however, if she calls and finds no help. If, however, she is met with more than perfunctory assistance—more than mere damage control—her mood will rise significantly. Responding to complaints is your opportunity to build and strengthen a positive relationship with your customer.

Convey Competence and Commitment

Your customer is calling in a state of at least some anxiety and at least some anger. He needs to hear four things from you and hear them right away:

First, that you understand.
Second, that you are sorry.
Third, that you are committed to help.
Fourth, that you are competent to help.

To get to the point at which you can deliver these messages credibly, you have to listen to the complaint, gathering as much information as you can. Next, respond by:

1. Demonstrating that you understand the complaint.
2. Promising that you will help.
3. Expressing empathy, understanding, and concern: "We're sorry that this has happened."
4. Providing a clearly competent plan of action.

If you believe you can fix the problem during this phone call, tell the caller what you propose to do. Walk him through whatever steps he needs to take to address the issue (see Chapter 16).

If the problem cannot be corrected by a customer procedure, give the caller explicit instructions for securing repair, replacement, or adjustment. If the customer has a range of options to choose from, present them. Explain all necessary procedures, including not only what you are asking the customer to do, but what you (and your company) will do. Close the call by apologizing. Do not make dramatic protestations of guilt. Instead, offer the apology as a springboard that concludes the call on an upbeat note. Convey your gratitude for the customer's patience and understanding.

The Customer Isn't Always Right

Not every customer complaint is factually valid. In other words, the customer is not *always* right. Despite this truth, your goal must be to avoid making the customer feel that he was wrong to choose your company or its product.

Never argue with the customer or browbeat him into admitting he is wrong. Instead, educate him so thoroughly and pleasantly that when the call is concluded, he hangs up thoroughly pleased that what he thought was a terrible problem has been solved both painlessly and efficiently. Do it this way:

1. Make clear that you appreciate your customer's concern.
2. Explain why the complaint is not valid. In doing this, keep your focus on the facts, not on the customer's judgment or lack thereof.
3. Continue the lesson by offering alternatives, including advice on how to use the product more effectively, sources of additional information, alternative products or accessories designed to make the product perform more nearly as the customer may wish, and so on.
4. You do not owe the caller an apology, because your company is not at fault. You may, however, wish to express your regret that the customer has been less than fully satisfied, but leaven this with an expression of hope that the alternative(s) you proposed will be of help.

If the caller won't give up and demands (for example) a refund, don't say no, but instead offer the most positive alternative available: "I cannot make a refund in this case, but I can offer you a 15 percent discount on a replacement part . . ."

Depending on your company's policies, you may be authorized to make a refund on the customer's request, regardless of the underlying facts ("no questions asked"). If this is the case, consider the refund an investment in goodwill. Make it graciously and without any judgmental comments.

THE USUAL SUSPECTS

Even with the best of merchandise, a lot can go wrong; however, the vast majority of complaints fall into a relatively small number of categories. The following are ideas for communicating effectively when dealing with the most common situations.

Wrong Item(s) Shipped

This may be the most common customer complaint. The reason is that, often, the error was the customer's and not the company's. Well, tuck that piece of information away in a corner of your consciousness and simply assume—or pretend to assume—that the customer is right.

1. Apologize.
2. Get the "right" information from the caller.
3. Confirm that information with the caller.
4. Tell the caller how to return the unwanted merchandise.
5. Close with a brief apology and thanks.
6. Above all, remember that your objective is to correct the error (regardless of who made it) and not to address the personality of the caller.

EXAMPLE

> CALLER: Hi there. This is Myron Jones. I ordered <item 1> but received <item 2>. You guys sent me something I don't want, don't need, and never asked for.
>
> YOU: I'm very sorry about that. Let's get it fixed right away.
>
> CALLER: Well, that's just it. I need <item 1> like yesterday . . .
>
> YOU: I completely understand. What I'm going to do is arrange for it to be cross-shipped, so we don't have to wait for you to return <item 2>. To do this, I need to confirm some information from you. First, we are delivering to <address>, correct?
>
> CALLER: Correct, yes.

> **YOU:** The item that you *want* is <item 1>, correct?
>
> **CALLER:** Absolutely.
>
> **YOU:** Got it. I can get that to you by <date>. We deliver to your area in the morning. Will someone be available to accept the delivery—because we will need a signature.
>
> **CALLER:** Yes, we'll be here.
>
> **YOU:** Great. So this is what I'd like to do: The driver who delivers <item 1> will also pick up <item 2> from you. That will save you time and trouble. Will you be able to have <item 2> packed back in its shipping box for our driver?
>
> **CALLER:** Yes, I can do that. No problem.
>
> **YOU:** Well, Mr. Jones, I am sorry for the error. I've just punched in the corrected order. Any questions?
>
> **CALLER:** No.
>
> **YOU:** Thank you for your patience and understanding, and have a great day.

Item Arrives Damaged

Receiving a damaged shipment creates disappointment and frustration. Acknowledge and address these feelings when you speak with the customer.

EXAMPLE

> **CALLER:** This is Paul Peters at Acme Electric. I've got a bad problem. We just took delivery on a <item>. Just unpacked it, and three parts are really banged up.
>
> **YOU:** Ouch! That's frustrating. I'm very sorry to hear it. Have you examined the whole shipment thoroughly? I don't want to increase your frustration, if you later find more damaged pieces. I can send a technician to your site to inspect the unit, if you like.
>
> **CALLER:** No, the damage is obvious, and I've unpacked everything.
>
> **YOU:** I understand. So, what parts do you need?
>
> **CALLER:** <Lists items.>

YOU: These parts *are* available for shipment overnight. If you prefer, however, I can dispatch an installer with them. First available for that option, however, is the day after tomorrow.

CALLER: I'm cool with installing them myself.

YOU: Then what we'll do is ship them to you in reusable packaging. So
once you've unpacked the replacements, just pack the damaged parts
in the boxes. You'll find shipping labels filled out. All we ask is that
you return the parts within seven days, so that we don't have to in-
voice you for the new parts.

CALLER: Fine.

YOU: Again, Mr. Peters, I'm sorry for the aggravation. Let's just confirm
the shipping information I have. <Confirms.> I appreciate your patience and understanding, and thanks for your business.

Product Defective or Does Not Perform as Expected

When a customer calls to report a defective or malfunctioning product, the
only assumption you should make is that—for *some* reason—the product has
failed to satisfy the customer. Do not argue about whether the product is defective or not. Instead, ask questions to discover the reasons for the product's
failure to provide satisfaction. Base your response on the customer's answers.
If *you* conclude that the product *is* defective, repair or replace it. If, however,
it is functioning properly, probe the reasons for the customer's dissatisfaction. Determine whether she is using the product correctly, and assess
whether her expectations are realistic or unrealistic. In your response, avoid
blame. Your only objective is to create satisfaction; therefore, consider the
alternatives available, such as exchanging this product for one that is more
appropriate to the customer's needs. This may be an upselling opportunity,
but be honest. Do not upsell the caller unless it is actually in her interest.

EXAMPLE

CALLER: My name is Sandra Murray. Yesterday, I purchased <product>
from <store>. I can't get it to work right, and I believe it's just defective.

YOU: I am very sorry you are having difficulty with it. I'm sure I can help. Please tell me what's going on. Can you describe the problem?

CALLER: [*Describes problem. It is apparent to you that the item is, in fact, defective.*]

YOU: Thank you. I understand now. Clearly, *you* aren't the problem! The unit itself is malfunctioning. We can solve this—and get you up and running as quickly as possible—in one of two ways. I can overnight a replacement for the <part>, which is not working. It will come with detailed directions for replacing it. This option will correct the problem most quickly. If you would rather not make the replacement yourself, however, you may return the entire unit to us. We will replace the defective part, test the unit, and return it to you, together with reimbursement for your shipping costs. That will take a week to turn around.

CALLER: How hard is it to replace the part?

YOU: Not hard at all, but some people just aren't comfortable doing these things themselves. It's a matter of personal choice.

CALLER: Well, I'd really rather have you folks do the work.

YOU: I understand. Ms. Murray, please pack the unit in its original carton with all of the original shipping material and ship it to us via <carrier>. The carton and the shipping material are designed to prevent damage. We will enclose a reimbursement check for shipping charges when we return the unit to you.

CALLER: I just have one more question. What happens if the new part doesn't resolve the problem?

YOU: We will test the unit before it leaves our facility, so I'm completely confident that the problem will be corrected. Is there anything else I can help you with today?

CALLER: No.

YOU: Again, Ms. Murray, I am very sorry that this happened. We'll get you up and running again just as soon as possible.

Complaint About a Service

Complaints about poor or inadequate service may be directed against Tech Support personnel, salespeople, or even Customer Service reps. When you receive complaints like these, you may find it a challenge to avoid taking sides or becoming defensive, especially if the complaint is directed against you, your department, or your friends and colleagues. Make every effort to take the professional approach—which means avoiding issues of personality or attitude and instead exclusively addressing issues. Ask questions designed to elicit the issues. Focus on them, and try to resolve them. The most effective procedure is to begin by acknowledging the complaint and listening to everything the customer has to say. Do not interrupt, unless you don't understand something. Only after the customer has finished her explanation should you respond. Do so this way:

1. Assure the customer that you understand and that you are committed to resolving the situation.
2. If there is an obvious and quick fix, propose it.
3. If you need to investigate the situation further—perhaps to talk to others involved—explain what you plan to do.
4. If appropriate at this point, apologize, but avoid focusing on any shortcomings or errors. Direct your apology at having failed to deliver absolute satisfaction.

EXAMPLE

CALLER: My name is Sharon Gallagher, and I'm sorry but I really have to complain about the absolutely terrible service I got from your Tech Support people. I'm just so angry about it . . .

YOU: I'm sorry to hear this. Please tell me exactly what happened.

CALLER: Well, I was put on hold immediately. Nobody got back to me for at least ten minutes. Finally, when a technician did get to me, he asked me a few questions, gave me some instructions, then told me to call back if the problem persisted. Of course, it *did* persist. So, once again, I called—was put on hold and so on. I'm upset.

YOU: I understand. Was the problem at least resolved?

CALLER: Well, yes . . .

YOU: That's good, at least. We actually devote a lot of training time to our Technical Support staff, and even though the problem was fixed, we do take any negative reports very seriously. I am going to have a conversation with the technician who took your call, then I will get back to you to discuss the outcome. Can you still be reached at 555-5555?

CALLER: Yes.

SERVICE: I should be back to you before the end of the week. Is that satisfactory?

CALLER: Yes.

YOU: Ms. Gallagher, I want to thank you for taking the time to call me about this. I will do everything I can to ensure that you are more satisfied in the future.

When you promise follow-up action and a follow-up call, do not fail to come through in a timely fashion. The follow-up might go something like this:

YOU: Ms. Gallagher, this is George Dabrowski from XYZ Customer Service. We spoke earlier in the week.

CUSTOMER: Yes, of course.

YOU: I had a conversation with Nat Goodwin, who is the tech representative who took your call, and, in fact, I have him on the line with us. Nat doesn't nor do I want to offer excuses to you. We both just want to apologize for giving you less than our best service. Nat was handling an unusually high volume of calls that day, which is why you were put on hold for what we both think was just too long a time. We're sorry we did not do a better job for you. Nat, anything to add?

NAT: Hello, Ms. Gallagher. I just wanted to add my apology. We did not give you the level of service you and all our customers deserve.

CUSTOMER: Well, I understand, and I appreciate your call.

YOU: We appreciate your understanding and patience. Have a great day.

Product Performance Is Disappointing

When a customer calls convinced that his purchase is not living up to its "hype," you need to confront a situation of acute dissatisfaction. After empathizing over the caller's disappointment, ask questions to determine if the product is defective, if the customer is using it correctly, and if the customer's expectations are appropriate and realistic.

If you determine that the product is not defective, and that the customer is using it correctly, and that his expectations are reasonable, your next task is to ascertain exactly how the product fails to meet them. Based on this, suggest a solution.

If you determine that the customer has unrealistic expectations about the product, consider suggesting alternative products more appropriate to the caller's desired application. If such alternatives are not available, explain the limitations of this type of product. If possible, offer workarounds that the caller may find helpful. If these are not available, suggest that the caller may have to adjust his expectations.

EXAMPLE

CALLER: This is Betty Lee. I'm calling from Port Royal. I recently purchased a <product> from you, and I'm just really, really disappointed with it.

YOU: I'm so sorry to hear that, Ms. Lee. So that I can understand what is at issue, can you tell me in what ways you are disappointed?

CALLER: I am using <product> to do <task 1>, and I have to say it does not do an adequate job.

You need to decide whether or not the product is designed to perform the task the caller has described. If it is clearly not an appropriate application, proceed this way:

YOU: Ms. Lee, the problem is that <product> was not designed for the application you describe. We do offer a <product 2>, which is intended for this kind of work. The fact is that if you mostly do <task 1>, you need to use <product 2>. What you have now will never do that job satisfactorily for you. It isn't designed to.

CALLER: So you're telling me I spent my money on the wrong thing?

YOU: What I'm saying is that the model you have now is for light-duty applications. It was not designed for <task 1>. Could you give me just a moment to call up your records on my computer screen?

CALLER: Yes . . . I'm *so* frustrated . . .

YOU: I do understand. Let me help. Just another few seconds. Okay: So, according to my records, you purchased <product> on <date>. Does that sound about right?

CALLER: It does.

YOU: Fortunately, we can give you full exchange value for <product> toward the purchase of <product 2>. Now, as I explained, <product 2> is specifically designed for the application you want—and will also do everything <product> does. It is a very good value at $XX. Make the exchange, and that will be a difference of $X.

CALLER: I appreciate it, but I really hate to spend more . . .

YOU: I can't blame you, but the fact is that the <product> you have now is simply not designed to do what you want it to do. <Product 2> is— and more. So at least you are getting excellent value for your money, and you are getting the right tool for the job. Naturally, whether you want to spend the additional money depends on just how important doing <task 1> is to you.

CALLER: It's what I need to do. So I'll exchange this for that.

If you determine that the product is performing correctly, the customer is using it correctly, and the application is appropriate, then you need to probe the source of the customer's dissatisfaction:

YOU: Okay. It's clear that <product> is functioning correctly, that you are using it correctly, and that you are using it to do what it's designed to do. I wonder if you could tell me a bit more about what you mean by "disappointed." In what ways is <product> falling short of what you expected?

CALLER: Mainly, I thought it would save me a lot more time than it does. It still takes me fifteen minutes to perform <task 1>.

YOU: Now I understand. Your unit is designed to perform <task 1>, but no product of this class can cycle faster that fifteen minutes. If this cycle time is a deal breaker for you, I can offer an upgrade trade-up to <product 2>, which is just about three times faster. As you might guess, however, it costs significantly more—nearly twice as much.

With trade-in of what you have, that will come to $XXX. Are you interested?

Technician Was Unable to Diagnose a Problem

When something goes wrong with a piece of technology, most of us take a quick fix for granted. When this fails to happen, we're upset—depending on circumstances, we may even be a bit panic-stricken. Put yourself in your customer's place. What do you feel—right now—about the people who sold you the costly hunk of junk sitting in inert silence after an authorized tech spent hours laboring over it only to come up with exactly nothing?

When you are confronted with a caller in this situation, resist making the customer's mistake of taking a quick fix for granted. Have a contingency plan ready for those occasions when, for whatever reason, your technical staff is unable to effect a quick repair. Your plan should include giving the customer the feeling that you are in competent control of the situation, and it should focus on getting the customer up and running as soon as possible. If at all possible, be prepared to dispatch a higher-level technician-adviser to the scene. Another option is to locate, secure, and install a "loaner" machine while the customer's device is down. If company policy and warranty terms permit, offer to replace rather than repair the unit.

Avoid either defending or denigrating the product. Work the problem—which is getting the customer back up and running. That should be your exclusive focus.

EXAMPLE

> CALLER: Look, your technician has been here half the day and still can't figure out what's wrong with my <product>. You've got to do something about this! I can't afford this downtime!
>
> YOU: I am very sorry that the service call is taking more time than either of us would like. In most cases, the technician is fully equipped to do diagnosis and repair on his own. But each situation is different, and the fact is that diagnosis is not always straightforward. Instead of eat-

ing up more of your productive time, I'm sending in Art Frankel, from our senior technical staff. He is a supervisor. This is our standard escalation procedure.

CALLER: How much longer is *this* going to take? I need this machine up and running!

YOU: I fully understand. If Art can't diagnose the problem by the end of your workday today, I will arrange to install a loaner unit tomorrow. It can be operational by ten. So, in the very worst case, that's when you'll be up and running—about ten tomorrow.

CALLER: Well, that's better than nothing. But I'm losing time *today*. Are you guys gonna compensate me for that? I mean, I do an awful lot of business with you.

YOU: I know, and we appreciate that business. None of us wants to see you have *any* downtime. I can promise you that you'll be up and running as soon as possible. If it is not before close of business today, then it will be by ten tomorrow morning. I can promise you that.

Repairs Fail

A product fails, is sent in for repair, and is returned—only to fail again. The customer is in a rage, not just at you and your company, but—worst of all—at herself, for having bought a bad piece of hardware from you. She's also scared—worried that now that your company has her money, you will leave her with a malfunctioning pile of circuit boards.

Recognize the fear and the anger. Begin by addressing these. That means conveying your absolute assurance that you will stand by the customer. Make it clear that the problem is not *hers* alone. It is a problem you willingly share with her. You are partners in solving it.

EXAMPLE

CALLER: I shipped my <product> back to you for warranty repairs last week. I've had it back here for a day—and this morning I've got *exactly* the same problem.

YOU: I'm sorry to hear that . . .

CALLER (*INTERRUPTING*): This is ridiculous. It is *costing* me downtime. I've never heard of something like this. Just send me a new unit—overnight.

YOU: I understand your frustration, and I appreciate the urgency of the situation. I will work with you to get you up and running as quickly as possible. Look, my name is Jane Finn. You are?

CALLER: Max Plummer.

YOU: May I call you Max?

CALLER: Sure . . .

YOU: Max, give me about ten seconds to get your service record up on my screen. I'm typing in the search request now, and it's coming up. You sent the unit in and we did <describe procedures>. The notes here say that the problem you described when you returned the unit for repair was <describes problem>. Is this accurate?

CALLER: Yes, yes—and the point is it's *not* fixed.

YOU: Did the unit function properly when it first came back to you?

CALLER: For a little while.

YOU: So—what?—for just about a day?

CALLER: Well, for maybe six or seven hours.

YOU: Here's what I can do. I will send a technician out today—to your site. He should be there in about two hours. He will bring with him a loaner unit. He'll install it, to get you up and running right away. If you can give him an out-of-the-way place to work, he'll see if he can address the issue with your unit right there at your location. If not, he'll leave you with the loaner and take your unit in to our facility. We'll do whatever is necessary to make it right—up to and including full replacement, if that is necessary. How does this sound to you?

CALLER: Can he get here any faster?

YOU: Unfortunately, given the distance involved, no.

CALLER: And how do I know I won't get the same failure again?

YOU: We will work until we've got it right. If we aren't satisfied, we'll replace the unit. In the meantime, you will be using the loaner, so production time lost will be held to a strict minimum. I wish it could be zero, but we'll do whatever is possible.

WORDS AND PHRASES TO USE

Answer

Can you describe the problem?

Complete satisfaction

Expedite

Facilitate

Fast track

First priority

Fix

Highest priority

I agree/appreciate/comprehend/
    hear you/understand

I'm here to help

Let's get this resolved together

Please describe the problem

Remedy

Repair

Satisfaction

Tell me what's happening

Test/tested

We stand behind

We will certify/solve this
    together/test

We won't quit on you

What would you like to see
    happen next?

You must be satisfied for us to be
    satisfied

WORDS AND PHRASES TO AVOID

Calm down

Don't worry

I just don't believe you

I'm afraid that's your problem

It's not so bad

Never heard that before

Not our fault

Nothing I can do about that

Relax

That cannot be

That wasn't a good idea

That's impossible

These things happen

You can't expect miracles

You have made the wrong
    choice

You have to understand

You must be mistaken

You need to spend more

You should have

CHAPTER 18

Create Fans

According to a 2012 survey by DMG Consulting, 63 percent of companies use digital social media—Facebook, Twitter, and the like—as part of their customer service programs (www.destinationcrm.com/articles/Columns/Departments/The-Tipping-Point/Using-Social-Media-for-Customer-Service-81584.aspx). That percentage will certainly continue to rise sharply over the next few years. Obviously, social media is important to marketing (76 percent of enterprises make it a part of their marketing efforts), and at 63 percent, customer service is closing the gap on marketing. Nevertheless, asked to explain the actual *role* of social media in our customer service program, many of us are simply at a loss for words.

Let me offer a quick snapshot that explains it all. Just consider the following anecdote marketing guru Peter Shankman relates in his *Customer Service: New Rules for a Social Media World* (Que, 2011).

Shankman was about to give a speech at an Omni hotel in Florida. Just twenty minutes before show time, the hotel Wi-Fi suddenly went down. This meant that Shankman would not be able to show a YouTube video that was critical to his presentation. He immediately pulled out his Blackberry and sent a message to Twitter: "Dear Omni hotel: key lime pie: Win. Wifi: fail."

The message, of course, was accessible to anyone who followed Shankman's Tweets. Omni, which was monitoring social media, understood this, and management dispatched a technician to the lecture site within eight minutes. Shankman's speech was saved—and a grateful Shankman congratulated Omni customer service on Twitter, the very same platform he had used to complain.

As Shankman observed, the hotel knew how to play "by the new rules of customer service." Seeing an "opportunity to turn a complainer into a fan," management took steps to do just that, thereby turning "a small complaint into a huge win . . . while preventing it from becoming a big problem."

SOCIAL MEDIA: CROWD-SOURCING CUSTOMER SERVICE

Digital social media—especially (at this writing) Facebook and Twitter—is an extraordinary tool for doing great customer service. By monitoring Facebook and Twitter, plus Google alerts (http://news.google.com), any customer service operation in any company can listen to its customers and potential customers in real time. Do this, and you will hear complaints, compliments, and comments—not just about your company, but also about your competitors and your industry. Take the time and effort to set up thoughtful keyword filters, and you will receive a steady stream of relevant messages, including those like the one Shankman Tweeted about the failure of the Omni hotel's Wi-Fi. Such monitoring will put you in a position to respond—again, in real time or very close to it—to problems as well as to opportunities, and to do so in ways so direct and so personal that you will very likely turn complainers into fans and fans into fanatics. You will do this one customer at a time, of course, but that customer, in turn, because she is obviously connected to others on the social web—to prospects as well as current customers—will amplify and magnify the effect of each problem solved. This is how corporate reputations are built in a digitally connected world. This is how social media converts good, competent customer service into absolutely dynamite public relations. Some industries have caught on to the power of

Twitter more than others. Airlines, for example, are particularly responsive, since so many travelers—who typically have time on their hands—Tweet instantly about airline experiences, both good and bad. And a significant proportion of those who Tweet are celebrities, who have a lot of followers.

STRATEGIC IDEAS

The first social media strategy a customer service operation should adopt is simply to *have a strategy*. Despite the fact that social media has made the commercial landscape more competitive than ever and has made each company's reputation more vulnerable than ever—every complainer now owns his own personal digital megaphone—nearly two-thirds of Tweeters who have Tweeted about an unsatisfactory experience with a company never receive a response from the company in question. This means that while about two-thirds of companies *claim* to use social media in their customer service programs, the same number *fail* to follow through on complaints made through social media channels. In other words, a majority of companies, despite their claims to the contrary, have implemented no effective social media strategy for customer service.

This neglect and failure not only exposes a company's reputation to danger, it allows two tremendous opportunities to escape unexplored and unexploited over and over again:

1. The opportunity to know your customers and prospective customers intimately.
2. The opportunity to level the playing field on which you compete with the biggest, richest, most powerful companies. By knowing your customers and working with them interactively, often in real time, you can render *your* brand of customer service second to none.

Two Strategic Approaches

So let's assume you do decide to adopt a social media strategy for delivering customer service. You now have another strategic decision to make:

1. Should you use social media mainly to monitor the social web for complaints and problems, reacting to them only as necessary? Or—
2. Should you expand your use of social media proactively, always looking for ways to reach out to customers and prospective customers, even to those who don't complain?

The fact is that number two can be done while simultaneously pursuing strategy number one, and doing the two together does not require much more time and effort than doing either one by itself. Therefore, while it is important to think of the social web as the foundation of a twenty-first-century complaint department (as we do toward the end of the chapter), it is also a platform and a tool to extend your customer outreach proactively and positively, complaints or no complaints.

By now you already know that customer service issues tend to fall into one (or more) of three categories:

1. Problems, questions, and complaints concerning products and services.
2. Customer suggestions for improvements to products or services.
3. Upselling by Customer Service reps, and the general extension of the customer service function into sales by promoting accessories and other products related to an original purchase.

These categories constitute the very nature of customer service; therefore, it makes no sense to limit customer service *on the social web* to monitoring and addressing only number one in the list above. This said, while the social web does enable you to respond quickly and personally in all three areas, nowhere is it more important to do so than in the case of number one. The faster and more cordially you respond to a complaint, the better chance you have of turning a dissatisfied and possibly vengeful customer into a satisfied and potentially generous customer—a complainer into a fan. Moreover, because you heard about the complaint via the social web, you can safely assume that this particular customer is digitally well connected and routinely uses Facebook, Twitter, and similar sites to share her opinions with friends and followers. This makes it even more important that you respond to her quickly, cordially, and effectively.

If you can offer an immediate fix, do so. If a customer's pizza reached him cold, reply to his Tweet with the offer of another pizza—pronto and free. But even if the issue is more serious or complicated and therefore cannot be resolved immediately, take immediate action. Tweet back a telephone number or an email address, inviting the customer to conduct the conversation offline. Accompany this offer with an assurance that the customer's issue is important to you, and that you are committed to resolving the situation as quickly and fully as possible.

Response to Tweet:

Please email a description of the problem you are having to xyz.com/social. We promise to do our best to resolve it quickly and fully.

In customer service, your prime objective—your mission of choice—is always to turn a negative experience into a positive one, to salvage the imperiled customer relationship, and to generate constructive word of mouth. In a digitally connected world, this objective is amplified, magnified, and accelerated into turning a detractor into a fan.

Whether you resolve the issue immediately or through subsequent action, never fail to follow up with a quick personal message:

I am pleased to learn that we resolved your problem with <product>. Thanks for keeping in touch!

or

I hope we have satisfactorily solved your problem with <product>. Please email us at xyz.com to let us know. We want you happy!

Get Fast, Get Even Faster

Make it your business to know what's happening in your industry, among your competition, in all parts of your own company, and with your customers. Learn how to use Google alerts and any alert services offered by websites particularly relevant to your product, service, or industry. These days, everyone, no matter how big or how small, possesses the technology to get the most up-to-date information on any topics for which they set search and filtering parameters. Assume your customers and your competition both can get the same information you can. Now try to get it faster than either of them.

Collect Customer Data

When you make a sale, figure out ways to ask your customer to give you her email address, and secure the customer's permission to contact her with information *of interest to her*. Similarly, whenever your company Tweets information or posts something on Facebook or another social site, ask for it to be "liked" on Facebook and followed on Twitter.

At point of sale in a store, offer each customer a coupon or other item of value in exchange for providing an email address and permission to contact him with information of value to the customer.

Address Complaints Proactively

If your monitoring of the social web detects buzz about a hitherto unrecognized problem, resist the temptation to stick your head in the sand—or to wait for unhappy customers to start calling one at a time and then in droves. Instead:

1. Alert your management to the problem, along with any other personnel in the company who should know about it.
2. Quickly formulate a plan of action.
3. Implement that plan by reaching out to your email list and to your Facebook friends and Twitter followers.

The resulting message should be something like this:

A few of our customers have been telling us that Product X sometimes fails to reach full speed. If this happens to you, simply press the "Reset" button twice.

While repetition of this problem is rare, should your Product X repeatedly fail to reach full speed, please call Customer Service at 555-555-5555, and we will send you an appropriate fix right away. As our way of thanking you for your understanding in this matter, please use code 12345 when you place your next order with us. It will get you a 15 percent discount.

Remember, when things go wrong, an apology is important, but a fix is absolutely critical.

Reach Out with Value

When you're in business, you naturally think your job is to sell stuff. You are wrong. In truth, your number one job is to create an ever-growing body of loyal—preferably *fanatically* loyal—customers who buy stuff, repeatedly, and who, in turn, persuade others to buy stuff, too.

1. Use the social web to help people by offering information valuable to them.
2. Ideally, the information you offer should be strongly related to your products and services—but not necessarily.
3. The information you provide should be free, with absolutely no strings attached.
4. The information you provide should never look like—or *be*—a commercial. It should be valuable and interesting in itself. It should be friendly. It should be helpful. Your objective in providing the information is not to sell anything, but to create loyalty (which, of course, is the emotional climate in which sales are, sooner or later, created).

EXAMPLE

An "artisan" bread bakery offers a blog on its website and posts this:

KEEPING ARTISAN BREAD FRESHER LONGER

When we want to keep something fresh, we automatically open the fridge and toss it in. This is not way to treat really good bread, however. Refrigeration sucks out the moisture and actually makes the bread go stale sooner.

For bread, one day in the fridge equals *three* days at room temperature!

Your best move is to store fine bread at room temperature in a tightly closed package. A lot of folks use linen bags, because they can be drawn tightly closed.

Of course, you already know that not all breads are created equal. French bread can go stale after just a few hours. In fact, all crusty breads are at their very best on the same day you buy them. Not that you should discard dried-out crusty bread. It makes great croutons and terrific French toast.

Just because you shouldn't refrigerate bread doesn't mean you can't freeze it. If you absolutely must store bread for longer than a couple of days, freeze it.

Just wrap it in foil, then put it in a sealed plastic bag. That will prevent freezer burn. When you're ready to use it, defrost it at room temperature or wrap it in fresh aluminum foil and put it in a preheated oven for five minutes. Frozen bread can stay in your freezer for up to three months.

Yes, it's about bread. Yes, it will put the reader in a bread-buying frame of mind. Yes, it can be accompanied online by mouthwatering pictures of delicious artisan bread. But no, it doesn't try to sell a customer a single thing. It just provides useful information and thereby helps to create a loyal customer or prospectively loyal customer.

A Small Problem Is Big Trouble—and an Even Bigger Opportunity

On the social web, small problems—in themselves easily and cheaply fixed—tend to create disproportionately large problems if they are left unattended to. If you receive a complaint online—or you pick up a complaint as you monitor the web—reach out immediately. Apologize, yes, but most of all, go for a quick, proactive, voluntary, and gracious fix. Your objective is not merely to mollify the complainer, but to turn her into a social web fan of your company.

EXAMPLE

Sorry to hear that our sales associate forgot to take 10 percent off your tire purchase this morning. He feels so bad that to make you *both* feel better, we're taking 15 percent off and throwing in a free oil change. Just come by with this email and the credit card you used to make the purchase. We'll credit back your card 15 percent of the purchase price. If you're ready for the oil change at that time, we'll give it to you then. Otherwise, come on back again for that when you need it. Thanks for your understanding! And thanks for being a great customer!

Evaluating Your Social Media Strategy

Evaluating the effectiveness of your social media strategy is not a matter of rocket science or impressionistic guesswork. Just look at the numbers:

1. Complaints: Are the numbers decreasing?
2. Compliments: Are the numbers increasing?
3. Sales inquiries: Are the numbers increasing?
4. Upselling and accessory selling: Are the numbers increasing?
5. Response time to complaints: Is the average reply time improving?
6. Resolution of complaints: Is the level of satisfactory resolution rising?
7. Complaint telephone calls to Customer Service: Is this traffic decreasing?
8. Positive buzz online: Use Google alerts and other off-the-shelf online metrics to measure the volume of mentions of your company and its products and services over given spans of time. Is the volume of the buzz increasing?

If the numbers are not going your way, rethink and revise your social media strategies. If they are, keep doing what you're doing—or start doing even more of it.

If you can consistently create customer satisfaction online, in real time, through social media channels, you will not only save staff time and effort, you will demonstrate your personal dedication and transparency to your customers. You will demonstrate your savvy, sensitivity, and availability. You will prove that your customer is always uppermost in the collective consciousness of your company.

THE TWENTY-FIRST-CENTURY COMPLAINT DEPARTMENT

Not too long ago, Customer Service heard about complaints in one of three ways exclusively. Either a customer phoned in, wrote something unpleasant on a comment card, or—if truly motivated—dashed off a letter (or email) to the manager, the president, the CEO, or maybe even directly to Customer Service. Those days are by no means over, but *these* days, increasingly, the savviest of your customers are expressing themselves on the social web. Most importantly, they are not just expressing *themselves*, they are expressing themselves about *your* company.

In short, companies no longer have full, exclusive in-house control over the customer service function and therefore no longer have full, exclusive control over shaping and changing their customer relationships.

This may sound scary, but in fact, it is a situation that is also full of opportunity. As we have already observed, the social web gives every company unprecedented access to the consumer conversation about itself, its products and services, its marketplace, its competitors, and its industry. It's just that social networking is, more and more, making customer service a partially *self-service* process.

The downside *is* scary. Unhappy customers place negative comments on websites—including Twitter and Facebook, as well as consumer-oriented sites and forums, some specifically dedicated to your particular industry—for all the Internet to see.

The upside is exciting—because "for all the Internet to see" includes *you*. And if *you* monitor the relevant sites, you will be alerted in real time, or in as close to real time as possible, to problems that you can turn into opportunities.

1. Proactively offer community forums integrated with your website. Invite customers to air their comments and complaints. Some can be dealt with by other customers: "Yes, I've had that problem. It's easy to fix. Here's how . . ." But it is up to you to monitor all of the posts and deal with customer complaints quickly and effectively.

2. Identify the websites and forums relevant to your marketplace and your industry. Monitor these for comments and complaints. Reach out to customers who post on these sites. Offer help. Offer solutions.

3. Set up keyword monitoring with Facebook, Twitter, and Google alerts. Keywords should include your company name, product names, model names, and descriptive words of any common product issues you may already be aware of. Be sure to include common misspellings: If you are Smitherz Company, include "Smithers," "Smathers," "Smither," and so on. You can learn how to use these tools by visiting the appropriate Facebook, Twitter, and Google websites. Be sure to check out Twitter's TweetDeck (www.tweetdeck.com), which is a very convenient and flexible tool for listening to multiple consumer conversations about multiple relevant topics in real time.

Be aware that Facebook offers consumers the ability to post comments about particular companies, including yours. These can be a treasure trove of information useful in dealing with customer complaints. With its apps that enable users to integrate blogs with the iPhone, iPod, and virtually all other smartphone and portable devices, Twitter has made it easy for consumers to Tweet comments and complaints about products and services received from companies and to do so on-site and in real time.

EXAMPLE

You manage a busy restaurant. You are monitoring your TweetDeck feed when you see the following: "Stuck at the bar at Sloan's. Table isn't ready. Isn't that the point of a reservation?" This is happening in real time, so you know that you are dealing with a disappointed and dissatisfied customer who is in your establishment *right now*. You also know that he is active on Twitter. Many other Twitter followers are seeing this bad PR about your restaurant. Some may even be thinking, *I* hate *that. I* hate *having to wait when I make a reservation. I'm not going to Sloan's anytime soon.*

But precisely because this is in real time, you can do something that will turn this loss into a win.

Tweet back to this customer: "Sorry for the delay. Show this Tweet to the bartender. Have a drink on us!"

Next thing you see: "Sloan's just gave me a free drink. Makes the wait worth it. And it's a really cool bar!"

Done right, and with the aid of online tools that enable you to vigilantly listen in on the ongoing conversation among your customers, the social web can enable you to deliver the greatest value customer service can *ever* deliver. It can transform a problem into an opportunity and a complainer (with a digital megaphone) into a fan (with that very same digital megaphone). It can turn a loss into a win.

INDEX

ALSO AVAILABLE IN THE HOW TO SAY IT® SERIES...

HOW TO SAY IT® POCKET GUIDES